SCHOLASTIC

W9-BJN-546

Differentiated Activities for Teaching Key Comprehension Skills

40+ Ready-to-Go Reproducibles
That Help Students at Different Skill
Levels All Meet the Same Standards

Martin Lee and Marcia Miller

New York • Toronto • London • Auckland • Sydney
Mexico City • New Delhi • Hong Kong • Buenos Aires

Teaching *Resources*

Our sincere thanks go to Sarah Longhi for her clarity, guidance, and dedication to this project.

Poetry Credits: Page 63: "March" by Mildred Pittinger is reprinted from POETRY PLACE ANTHOLOGY. Copyright © 1983 by Edgell Communications by permission of Scholastic Inc.; Page 64: "March" by Elizabeth Coatsworth. From SUMMER GREEN by Elizabeth Coatsworth. Copyright © 1948 by Macmillan Publishing Co., Inc. and renewed 1968 by Elizabeth Coatsworth Beston.

Photo Credits: Page 27 © The Granger Collection; Page 28 © CORBIS; Pages 33 and 34 courtesy of www.skidboot.com; Page 45 © nimade/istockphoto; Page 46 © CW03070/istockphoto; Page 57 © topora/Shutterstock; Page 58 © Galyna Andrushko/Shutterstock

Editor: Sarah Longhi

Content editor: Nicole Iorio

Designer: Holly Grundon

Illustrator: Mike Moran

Cover designer: Maria Lilja

ISBN-13: 978-0-545-23452-8

ISBN-10: 0-545-23452-2

Contents

Activities

Introduction

Each child arrives in your classroom with a unique set of experiences, abilities, and needs. Prior knowledge, language skill, ability to focus, and other key factors vary widely in any grouping.

Given the challenge of helping all learners master core grade-level concepts and skills, how can you address a typical range of needs without creating 30 different plans per lesson per subject per day? You can differentiate your instruction, adjusting your presentation style and modifying the level of challenge for learners at several levels rather than expecting students to adapt themselves to a standard curriculum or method of teaching (Hall, 2002).

This book can be an effective tool to help you differentiate reading instruction. Each lesson opens with a passage for all students to read. (Passage selections include both fiction and nonfiction pieces that vary in genre and style.) After the passage, you'll find three leveled activity sheets, each offering comprehension and word-study questions that target important reading skills and strategies. As they complete their tiered activities, students move along different but related paths to actively process information and demonstrate learning. They read, think, respond, summarize, retell, write, explain, extrapolate, and create projects.

The chart below summarizes the key elements of differentiated instruction. We use the acronym *CAP,* for **C**ontent, **A**pproach, and **P**roduct. Teachers *plan CAP*; students *perform CAP*. For each tier, notice what the teacher does and what students do.

TEACHERS	"CAP"	STUDENTS
Select materials Set goals Prepare lessons	**CONTENT** *Consistent for all*	Choose materials Understand objectives Clarify expectations
Make groupings Address modalities Vary pacing Provide support	**APPROACH** *Differentiate as needed*	Get involved Apply skills Develop strategies Sharpen techniques
Develop activities Make adjustments Wrap up the experience Extend	**PRODUCT** *Ideal for differentiation*	Present projects Participate in discussion Perform assessment Reflect on learning

Differentiated instruction isn't a single strategy. Rather, this flexible and research-based approach incorporates many strategies to better serve student diversity. In *Integrating Differentiated Instruction and Understanding by Design,* Carol Ann Tomlinson and Jay McTighe state that differentiated instruction "…focuses on whom we teach, where we teach, and how we teach" (2006).

Using This Book

In developing this book, we have used the *CAP* model as a structural guideline to streamline your efforts to differentiate instruction. We hope the lessons will serve as tools to empower you to become more familiar and comfortable with implementing tiered activities.

Here is how we suggest you use this book:

Each lesson begins with *content* that is consistent for all students, in the form of a two-page reading passage. We have selected topics and genres that support the goals and tasks described on the teacher page. In previewing, reading, and discussing the reading passage with the whole class, you guide students to clarify objectives and expectations.

Our *approach* is to have students complete one of the three leveled activity Sheets developed for that reading passage. Each level is identified throughout the book by its own recurring icon.

    ◆ Tier 1 is best used with struggling learners.

    ● Tier 2 is intended for use with students who are performing on level.

    ⬟ Tier 3 is designed to challenge more advanced students.

As students work through the activity sheets individually, in pairs, or in small groups, they interact with the passage, applying skills, developing strategies, and sharpening their techniques for completing the tasks. The accompanying teacher page offers ideas to guide you as you prepare the lesson. It suggests how to encourage and support students in each tier. Each activity sheet also presents Word Work, a word-study activity designed to help students be attentive to word parts, word patterns, and grammatical structure as they read.

The *product* for each lesson is a blend of the written responses to questions, the Word Work tasks, and the response to a multiple-choice item about the passage. It might also include one or more of the reading response activities at the back of the book, as well as students' participation in discussion and their reflections on their work. We hope that the selections themselves may inspire you to add your own ideas so that you can further engage your students as they extend their learning.

Keep in mind that the key to successful differentiated instruction is to know your students.

    ❖ Observe early and often to determine *how* to differentiate, and whether the approaches you've presented are working.

Each Lesson Includes:

TEACHER PAGE

READING PASSAGE

TIER 1 PAGE

TIER 2 PAGE

TIER 3 PAGE

Sources:

Gregory, G. H. &
Chapman, C. (2002).
*Differentiated instructional
strategies:
One size doesn't fit all.*
Thousand Oaks, CA:
Corwin Press.

Hall, T. (2002).
Differentiated instruction.
Wakefield, MA:
National Center on
Accessing the General
Curriculum. Retrieved
from http://www.cast.org/
publications/ncac/ncac_
diffinstruc.html

Heacox, D. (2002).
*Differentiating instruction
in the regular classroom:
How to reach and teach
all learners, grades 3–12.*
Minneapolis, MN: Free
Spirit Publications.

Tomlinson, C. A. &
McTighe, J. (2006).
*Integrating differentiated
instruction & understanding
by design.* Alexandria,
VA: Association for
Supervision and
Curriculum Development.

❖ Be flexible! Adjust and adapt grouping, pacing, modalities, and support as needed.

❖ Encourage and model active reading. Suggest that students jot down ideas on sticky notes, circle or underline hard words, sketch scenes for clarity and visualization, or take margin notes. To support struggling readers, echo-read some passages, or record the passage so they can listen and follow along in the text. Model techniques to unlock new vocabulary.

❖ Mix and match tasks, presentations, or activities within tiers to better fit your students' abilities and interests.

❖ Help students make good choices that can propel their learning. For example, suggest that struggling writers use graphic organizers, highlighter pens, or peer-partner chats. Advanced learners might debate solutions, research additional data, or pursue tangential ideas.

❖ Expect students to demonstrate learning at their own level. Ideally, differentiated instruction should provide ample challenge to stimulate students to work and succeed, but not so much as to cause them stress or lead them to a point of frustration.

❖ Provide feedback as often as possible while students work; invite them to express their thinking or explain their solution strategies.

❖ Encourage self-assessment to empower students to identify their own strengths and weaknesses. This can lead students to deeper ownership of their responsibilities as learners.

Reading Standards Correlation Grid

Although there are varied standards to guide reading comprehension instruction, we present here a streamlined version to identify which major skills have been addressed in each lesson. The lessons align with the Standards for the English Language Arts created by the International Reading Association and the National Council of Teacher of English (see www.reading.org), with focus on the following:

❖ Students read a wide range of print and nonprint texts to build an understanding of texts, of themselves, and of the cultures of the United States and the world; to acquire new information; to respond to the needs and demands of society and the workplace; and for personal fulfillment. Among these texts are fiction and nonfiction, classic and contemporary works.

❖ Students apply a wide range of strategies to comprehend, interpret, evaluate, and appreciate texts. They draw on their prior experience, their interactions with other readers and writers, their knowledge of word meaning and of other texts, their word identification strategies, and their understanding of textual features (e.g., sound-letter correspondence, sentence structure, context graphics).

We have also aligned our lessons to the McREL Content Knowledge standards for language arts (see www.mcrel.org/compendium) and the overarching reading standards:

❖ Uses the general skills and strategies of the reading process

❖ Uses reading skills and strategies to understand and interpret a variety of literary texts

❖ Uses reading skills and strategies to understand and interpret a variety of informational texts

	Set a Purpose for Reading	Recognize Author's Purpose/Point of View	Understand Literary Elements	Identify Main Idea and Supporting Details	Analyze Text Elements and Structures	Compare and Contrast	Recognize Cause and Effect	Differentiate Between Fact and Opinion	Identify Symbolism and Figurative Language	Summarize	Make Connections	Draw Conclusions and Make Inferences	Sequence Events.
1. Making a Bird Feeder	✔				✔		✔					✔	✔
2. Clown Rounds			✔			✔	✔	✔		✔	✔	✔	
3. A Pair of Parties	✔			✔	✔	✔						✔	✔
4. Teacher Boy			✔			✔	✔				✔	✔	
5. Rascal of the Ranch	✔	✔				✔	✔	✔			✔	✔	✔
6. The Giant Hairy Toe		✔	✔	✔		✔	✔		✔	✔		✔	✔
7. The Echidna	✔			✔	✔	✔	✔			✔		✔	
8. Goal!			✔		✔	✔	✔	✔		✔		✔	
9. Amber	✔			✔						✔		✔	✔
10. Three Poems		✔			✔	✔			✔	✔		✔	
11. Meet a Book	✔			✔	✔	✔					✔	✔	✔

Teaching
Making a Bird Feeder

Students follow instructions for making a simple bird feeder.

Tasks	Tier 1 Below Level	Tier 2 On Level	Tier 3 Above Level
Set a purpose for reading	X	X	X
Use text structures: how-to text	X	X	X
Draw conclusions	X	X	X
Use prepositions to show position	X	X	X

Getting Started

See the tips below for introducing the lesson. Make copies of the reading passage (pages 9–10) and the appropriate leveled activity sheet for each group of learners (pages 11–13).

Access prior knowledge by discussing what students know about how to follow an ordered list of instructions. Build background on bird feeders and bird food.

Tier 1

- **Set a Purpose for Reading:** Discuss that this is a how-to passage. It provides the steps to follow, in correct order, to complete a task. Check that students understand what the outcome should be.

- **Use Text Structure:** Talk about how this selection looks different from other kinds of writing students have read. Direct them to notice the three main sections: introduction, materials list, and directions in steps. Ask them how each list is organized (by items needed; in number order).

- **Draw Conclusions:** For item 3, have students tell what might happen if the steps were not numbered.

- **Word Work:** Work through this section with the group. Extend by inviting students to identify other position words found in the selection and to use them in meaningful sentences.

Tier 2

- **Use Text Structure:** Ask students to describe how this selection looks different from other kinds of writing they have read. Ask them to tell how they know to gather materials *before* they follow the steps.

- **Draw Conclusions:** Ask students what could happen if the steps for making the bird feeder were given in the wrong order or if any steps were left out altogether.

- **Word Work:** Work through this section with the group. Extend by asking students to formulate their own sentences for the two words *not* used in the answers.

Tier 3

- **Use Text Structure:** Compare and contrast bulleted lists with numbered lists. Ask students to explain why the materials needed are *not* numbered while the steps listed are numbered.

- **Draw Conclusions:** For item 4, ask: *What can you conclude about how birds respond to seeds?*

- **Word Work:** Have students share their sentences. Challenge them to identify other position words that do *not* appear in the selection. Ask volunteers to use these in original sentences.

Skills:
• Setting a purpose for reading
• Analyzing text structures
• Drawing conclusions

Making a Bird Feeder:
Reading Passage

Here is an in idea for a simple bird feeder you can make yourself. It is easy to make, and it doesn't cost much. It works, too! First, collect everything you need.

You Need

- string or twine
- large pinecone
- butter knife
- vegetable shortening
- birdseed
- aluminum foil or waxed paper

You are ready to go when you have all these things.

Steps to Follow

Use the pictures to help you.

1. Loop a long piece of string or twine around the top of a large pinecone. Tie a knot to make a hanging loop.

2. Use a butter knife to smear shortening all over the pinecone. Spread it in between the scales, too.

(continued)

Making a Bird Feeder: Reading Passage

3. Sprinkle birdseed onto a piece of foil or waxed paper. Spread the seeds without getting too close to the edges.

4. Roll your messy pinecone in the birdseed. Press down to help the seeds stick. Roll until the pinecone is coated with seeds.

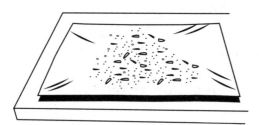

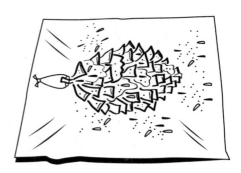

5. Your bird feeder is done! Hang it on a tree branch or fence. Put it high up so your pets won't get at it. Then clean up your mess.

6. Wait for hungry birds to come by. Watch them peck away at the tasty treat you made!

 Differentiated Activities for Teaching Key Comprehension Skills: Grades 2–3 © 2010 by Martin Lee and Marcia Miller. Scholastic Teaching Resources

Making a Bird Feeder: Activity Sheet

(Read and Understand) Read the passage. Then answer these questions.

1. What will you learn to do by reading this piece? _____

2. Circle the materials you need to have to make a bird feeder.

3. You will follow steps to make a bird feeder.

How many steps are there? _____

Why are the steps numbered? _____

4. When do you use the butter knife? Underline that step.

(Word Work: Position Words)

Some words describe position and relationship. Here are four from the piece:

from   with   near   up

Write each word in the sentence where it belongs.

I got a butter knife _____ the kitchen.

A bird was flying _____ in the sky.

I keep my slippers _____ my bed.

I drink milk _____ my toast.

(Check) Circle the best choice.

Why do you use the butter knife?

A. to hang the bird feeder

B. to roll the pinecone in the seeds

C. to smear shortening on the pinecone

D. to cut the foil or waxed paper

Name _____   Date _____

 # Making a Bird Feeder: Activity Sheet

Read the passage. Then answer these questions.

1. What will you learn to do by reading this piece? _____

2. What part of the passage tells you what materials you need? _____

_____

3. Which step tells how you will use the knife? _____

4. You hang up the bird feeder when it is done. How do you know when it is finished?

_____

(**Word Work: Position Words**)

Some words show position. Here are six from the piece:

out   with   near   up   around   from

Write each word in the sentence where it belongs.

I got a butter knife _____ the kitchen.

I looked _____ in the sky and saw a bird.

I keep my slippers _____ my bed.

Ice cream melts if you leave it _____.

The fire station is _____ the corner from the school.

(**Check**) Circle the best choice.

Why do you need string?

A. to attach birdseed to the pinecone   C. to hold the butter knife

B. to hang up the bird feeder   D. to tie pinecones together

Differentiated Activities for Teaching Key Comprehension Skills: Grades 2–3 © 2010 by Martin Lee and Marcia Miller. Scholastic Teaching Resources

Name _____   Date _____

 # Making a Bird Feeder: Activity Sheet

Read and Understand) Read the passage. Then answer these questions.

1. What makes this a how-to passage? _____

2. What do you need to do before you start making the bird feeder? _____

_____

3. Why do you need string? _____

4. How do you know when your bird feeder is finished? _____

_____

Word Work: Position Words

Some words show position or relationships.

For each position word, write a sentence about birds.

out: _____

near : _____

down : _____

from : _____

Check) Circle the best choice.

Why do you use the shortening?

A. to hang the bird feeder

B. to make the birdseed stick to the pinecone

C. to make a knot at the top of the cone

D. to eat while making the bird feeder

Teaching **Clown Rounds**

Students read a humorous story about clowns in a hospital.

Skills:

- Summarizing and making connections
- Comparing and contrasting
- Making inferences

Tasks	Tier 1 Below Level	Tier 2 On Level	Tier 3 Above Level
Summarize and make connections	X	X	X
Compare and contrast characters	X	X	X
Make inferences	X	X	X
Link pronouns with their antecedents	X	X	X

Getting Started

See the tips below for introducing the lesson. Make copies of the reading passage (pages 15–16) and the appropriate leveled activity sheet for each group of learners (pages 17–19).

Access prior knowledge by discussing where clowns usually perform and who the usual people are who work or volunteer in hospitals.

 ## Tier 1

- **Make Connections and Summarize:** Discuss the concept that joking and laughter can help someone who is nervous or scared of something. Ask students to share experiences with this kind of humor. Then have them summarize the clowns' role in the story and describe how the students themselves might react if they were in a similar situation.

- **Make Inferences** Ask: *What does the nurse mean by calling Dr. Tickles a "special" doctor?*

- **Compare and Contrast:** For items 3 and 4, have students compare the outfits worn by the two clowns with the clothes real doctors and nurses wear.

- **Word Work:** If necessary, define *noun* as a word that names a person, place, thing, or idea, and *pronoun* as a word that takes the place of a noun.

 ## Tier 2

- **Make Connections and Summarize:** Have students summarize what happens during this part of Toby's hospital visit. Then have them discuss what might cheer them up if they were in a hospital, including how they would react to a visit from clowns.

- **Make Inferences** Ask students to tell how Toby's visitors' names reveal that they are clowns. Ask them to tell what the first nurse meant by saying that Dr. Tickles is a "special" doctor.

- **Compare and Contrast:** For item 4, have students compare and contrast the different ways that clowns and doctors can make you feel better.

- **Word Work:** If necessary, define *noun* as a word that names a person, place, thing, or idea, and *pronoun* as a word that takes the place of a noun.

 ## Tier 3

- **Make Connections and Summarize:** Challenge students to suggest other possible names for clowns who act as doctors and nurses.

- **Compare and Contrast:** For item 4, have students compare and contrast things that clowns and doctors may do to make a person feel better.

- **Word Work:** Introduce the pronouns *him*, *her*, *us*, and *them*. Ask students to say sentences that use those pronouns, and to identify the noun (antecedent) that each refers to.

Skills:
- Summarizing and making connections
- Comparing and contrasting
- Making inferences

Clown Rounds:
Reading Passage

It was morning in the hospital. Toby was awake. He was worried. He was having an operation that day.

A nurse came in. "Hi, Toby. Dr. Tickles is here to see you."

"But my doctor is Dr. Wong," said Toby.

The nurse winked. "Dr. Tickles is a special doctor."

Toby heard a loud honk. A doctor came in. His white coat was covered in patches. He wore big purple glasses. He had on a blue wig and a red nose. He had a squeeze horn.

"Hey, Toby. I'm Dr. Tickles!" Toby's eyes opened wide.

"You're not a doctor. You're a clown!"

"Right! Eyes perfect!" Dr. Tickles honked his horn. "Now, smile!"

Toby forced a smile.

"Good grin. Teeth perfect!" Dr. Tickles honked again. "Toby, I make clown rounds," he said. "I check you. I answer questions. I also do cool stuff. Let me hear your heart."

Dr. Tickles took out a huge stethoscope. He put it on Toby's right elbow. "No beats!"

Toby giggled, "My heart's not there!"

"Oops. Sorry. So it's your turn," said Dr. Tickles. "Ask me anything."

(continued)

Clown Rounds: Reading Passage

(continued)

Toby frowned. "Do I really need this operation?"

Dr. Tickles looked hard at Toby. "Dr. Wong says it will make you feel better." Then he blew up a long balloon and tied it into a goofy hat. He plopped the hat on Toby's head. "Perfect! Nurse Boo-Boo, I need you!"

Squish, squash! Nurse Boo-Boo jumped into the room. Her white shoes squeaked. She wore a baseball cap with bandages on it. She held a giant needle. Toby gasped, and then smiled. It wasn't a real needle. It was a balloon. "Say ahhhh," she said. Nurse Boo-Boo poked Toby's arms, yelling "Ouch! Ouch!" Toby laughed.

Then she took out a squirt lemon. She squirted it into the air to test it. "Use this if you feel sour!" she said. She gave the squirt lemon to Toby. He squirted the doctor and nurse. Soon, all three were laughing. Dr. Tickles did magic tricks. Nurse Boo-Boo juggled cups. Toby made animal noises. There was no time to worry.

Then Dr. Wong came in. "A word please, Dr. Tickles?" she said. The real doctor took the clown doctor into the hall. Nurse Boo-Boo and Toby waited, still giggling.

Dr. Tickles came back and said, "Your funny bone, smiler, and laugher work just fine. Your parents are here. And you're ready for your operation." Dr. Tickles and Nurse Boo-Boo hugged Toby. "Don't squirt Dr. Wong," they whispered as they left.

Clown Rounds: Activity Sheet

(Read and Understand) Read the passage. Then answer these questions.

1. What are the names of the two clowns? _____

2. Why did the clowns visit Toby that morning? _____

_____

3. Dr. Tickles is not really a doctor. Circle three clues that tell you this.

4. How do you know that Nurse Boo-Boo is not a real nurse? _____

_____

Circle two paragraphs that tell you this.

> *She* and *doctor* name the same person.

(Word Work: Pronouns) Read these two sentences:

A <u>doctor</u> came into the room.   (She) came into the room.

Read the first sentence. Look for the underlined word.
Circle the word in the second sentence that names the same person or thing.

<u>Toby</u> was sick.	He was sick.
The <u>stethoscope</u> felt cold.	It felt cold.
Where is <u>Nurse Boo-Boo</u>?	Where is she?
<u>Mom and Dad</u> visited.	They visited.

(Check) Circle the best choice.

Why do Dr. Tickles and Nurse Boo-Boo visit kids in the hospital?

A. to give them medicine   C. to cheer them up

B. to listen to their heartbeats   D. to figure out what is wrong with them

Clown Rounds: Activity Sheet

Read and Understand Read the passage. Then answer these questions.

1. Why did the clowns visit Toby that morning? _____

_____

2. How do you know that Dr. Tickles is not a real doctor? _____

_____

3. What tells you that Nurse Boo-Boo is not a real nurse? _____

_____

4. In what way do you think doctors and clowns are alike? _____

_____

Word Work: Pronouns

Read the first sentence. Then choose a word from the box to complete the second sentence.

It	They	He	She

My mother visited me.   _____ visited me.

Toby needs an operation.   _____ needs an operation.

The needle was really a balloon.   _____ was really a balloon.

Dr. Tickles and Nurse Boo-Boo visited.   _____ visited.

Check Circle the best choice.

How do you know that the clowns cheered up Toby?

A. Dr. Wong came into the room.   C. Toby giggled and made animal noises.

B. Toby's elbow had a heartbeat.   D. The clowns operated on him.

Name _____   Date _____

 # Clown Rounds: Activity Sheet

Read and Understand Read the passage. Then answer these questions.

1. Why did the clowns visit Toby that morning? _____

_____

2. How do you know that Dr. Tickles is not a real doctor? _____

_____

3. What tells you that Nurse Boo-Boo is not a real nurse? _____

_____

4. In what way do you think doctors and clowns are alike? _____

_____

Word Work: Pronouns

Read the first sentence. Then write a pronoun in the second
sentence so that it means the same thing.

Dr. Sarah Wong spoke to my parents.	_____ spoke to my parents.
The boy needs an operation.	_____ needs an operation.
The stethoscope was really a toy.	_____ was really a toy.
Dr. Tickles and Nurse Boo-Boo visited Toby.	_____ visited Toby.

Check Circle the best choice.

How do you know that the clowns cheered up Toby?

A. Toby didn't squirt Dr. Wong.

B. Toby's elbow did not have a heartbeat.

C. Toby giggled and made animal noises.

D. Toby's parents let the clowns do the operation.

Teaching **A Pair of Parties**

Students read two different styles of party invitations.

Tasks	◆ Tier 1 Below Level	● Tier 2 On Level	⬠ Tier 3 Above Level
Set a purpose for reading	X	X	X
Compare and contrast	X	X	X
Identify main ideas and details		X	X
Make inferences	X	X	X
Capitalize proper nouns	X	X	X
Use abbreviations			X

Getting Started

See the tips below for introducing the lesson. Make copies of the reading passage (pages 21–22) and the appropriate leveled activity sheet for each group of learners (pages 23–25).

Access prior knowledge by talking about different kinds and styles of party invitations. Review proper nouns, abbreviations, and proper-noun abbreviations

---

 ## Tier 1

- **Set a Purpose for Reading:** Ask students to tell what information they would expect to learn from a party invitation. Guide them to look for the use of these details in each invitation.

- **Compare and Contrast:** For item 1, ask students to explain how they know what kind of party each child is having.

- **Main Ideas and Details:** For item 3, ask: *What is the special way that Diana will identify her house on her party day?* For item 4, ask how they know that Duquan's party will be in a restaurant.

- **Word Work:** Ask students to explain why *street* and *avenue* are sometimes capitalized.

 ## Tier 2

- **Set a Purpose for Reading:** Ask students to tell what details they would expect to find in a party invitation.

- **Compare and Contrast:** Have small groups compare the styles of the two invitations. Ask them which invitation shows the key details more clearly, and to explain why.

- **Main Ideas and Details:** Ask students to tell which party comes first and by what date guests need to respond. For item 3, have them describe how Diana will identify her house on party day.

- **Word Work:** Discuss when *street* and *avenue* should be capitalized. Have students provide examples of each.

 ## Tier 3

- **Set a Purpose for Reading:** Ask: *What information would you expect to learn from a party invitation?*

- **Compare and Contrast:** Ask: *Which invitation do you think shows key details more clearly?*

- **Main Ideas and Details:** Ask students to tell by what date guests need to respond to the parties. For item 3, have them explain how they knew which was the three-hour party.

- **Make Inferences:** Have students explain their answers to item 4. Ask them to tell what they might wear and bring to the other party.

- **Word Work:** Point out that abbreviations of proper nouns need to begin with capital letters.

A Pair of Parties:
Reading Passage

Tameka is jumping for joy! She got invited to two different parties on the same weekend. Read the invitations she got in the mail.

Diana Pham invites you to a
POOL PARTY

Hello, swimmers!
Come over and enjoy summer with my family!

You can wade, float, splash, swim, and dive.
We'll play games like water tag, pool hoops, and octopus.

Date: Sunday, July 14

Start Time: 2 PM
We will swim for 2 hours. My dad will grill hot dogs and burgers at 4 PM. My mom will make her famous root beer floats. She calls them brown cows.
The party will end at 5 PM.

Place: 53 Poppy Rd.
It's the last brick house on the left. Look for balloons on the mailbox. Walk through the gate and go around to the back.

Bring: swim suit, towel.
We have pool toys, sunscreen, and blankets to lie on.

Please tell me if you can come.
Call me at 555-4321 by Friday, July 12, at the latest.

I really hope to see you in the pool. It will be a total SPLASH!

(continued)

You Are Invited!

Host: Duquan Monroe

What: Birthday Party

Date: Saturday, July 13

Time: Noon to 2 PM

Place: The Pizza Palace
397 State St.
Upstairs party room

Wear: Play clothes

More Details: Duquan is turning 9—so fine!

Gift Ideas: Duquan loves sharks. He also likes science, sports, art, and magic tricks.

There will be games, contests, music, prizes, pizza, and birthday cake. (There will be sandwiches for kids who don't like pizza.)

Can You Come?

RSVP *YES or NO.* Call 555-6789.
Please respond by Wednesday, July 10.

A Pair of Parties: Activity Sheet

Read and Understand Read the passage. Then answer these questions.

1. Who is having a pool party? _____

   Who is having a pizza party? _____

2. Circle the date of each party on the reading passage pages.

   Whose party is on a Saturday? _____

3. How do you find Diana's house? Circle the paragraph that tells you.

4. Whose party will be in a restaurant? _____

Word Work: Proper Nouns

Look at the invitations. Find and circle:

A girl's name

The name of a street

The name of a restaurant

A day of the week

 Tip

Names start with capital letters. They are *proper nouns*.

Example:

Mr. Adams   **Mott Road**   **King School**
Central Park   **Red River**

Check Circle the best choice.

Which gift would Duquan probably like most?

A. pool toys

B. pizza

C. a T-shirt

D. a magic set

A Pair of Parties: Activity Sheet

Read and Understand Read the passage. Then answer these questions.

1. Is Diana having a party at home or out? _____

Is Duquan having a party at home or out? _____

2. Whose party is on a Saturday? _____

3. How do guests find Diana's house? _____

_____

4. What is a "brown cow"? _____

Word Work: Proper Nouns

Look at the invitations. Find and circle:

A girl's name

The name of a street

The name of a restaurant

A day of the week

 Tip

Names start with capital letters. They are *proper nouns*.

Example:

Mr. **A**dams	**M**ott **R**oad	**K**ing **S**chool
Central **P**ark	**R**ed **R**iver	

Check Circle the best choice.

Which gift would Duquan probably like most?

A. a bathing suit

B. a brown cow

C. a fish tank

D. a pizza pan

Name _____ Date _____

 # A Pair of Parties: Activity Sheet

Read and Understand Read the passage. Then answer these questions.

1. Who is having a party at home? _____

Who is having a party in a restaurant? _____

2. You want to go to Duquan's party. By what day must you let him know?

_____

3. Whose party will happen first? _____

Whose party will last for three hours? _____

4. You wear jeans and a T-shirt. You bring a gift of a magic kit.

Whose party are you going to? _____

Word Work: Abbreviations Match each word with its abbreviation.

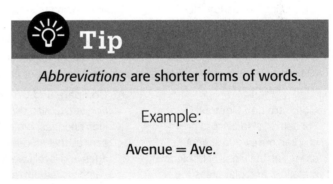

Word	Abbreviation
Mister	Bldg.
Street	Dr.
Doctor	Mr.
Wednesday	St.
Building	Wed.

Tip

Abbreviations are shorter forms of words.

Example:

Avenue = Ave.

Check Circle the best choice.

You call Diana and Duquan. Which question might you ask Diana?

A. What kinds of sandwiches will there be?

B. Do you already have a good book about fish?

C. Should I bring sunscreen?

D. How do you get to State Street?

Teaching **Teacher Boy**

Students read a story about children who attend a pioneer school.

Skills:

- Understanding narrative elements
- Drawing conclusions
- Comparing and contrasting

Tasks	◆ Tier 1 Below Level	● Tier 2 On Level	⬠ Tier 3 Above Level
Understand narrative elements	X	X	X
Draw conclusions	X	X	X
Compare and contrast	X	X	X
Use contractions	X	X	X

Getting Started

See the tips below for introducing the lesson. Make copies of the reading passage (pages 27–28) and the appropriate leveled activity sheet for each group of learners (pages 29–31).

Access prior knowledge by talking about what the class knows about the daily lives of pioneers. Build background on pioneer children and frontier schools

 Tier 1

- **Narrative Elements: Setting:** For item 1, guide children to clues that the story takes place in a small frontier community in the past. Discuss the concepts that during this period, all children helped out at home and were not required go to school. Explain that students of all ages and levels were in the same classroom.

- **Compare and Contrast:** For item 2, also discuss how children traveled to school, as well as the kinds of books, materials, and play areas the schools had then.

- **Narrative Elements: Problem and Solution:** Talk with students about why Jake took over. Ask them to tell what happens today when a teacher is late or absent at their school.

- **Word Work:** You may consider having students work in pairs on the table.

 Tier 2

- **Narrative Elements: Setting:** For item 1, guide children to clues that the story takes place in a small frontier community in the past. Clarify that, at that time, going to school was not compulsory. For item 3, have students describe what happens at their school when a teacher is late or absent.

- **Compare and Contrast:** For item 2, also discuss how kids and teachers got to their school, that students of all ages and levels were in the same classroom, and that pioneer schools had few books, materials, and play areas.

- **Draw Conclusions:** For item 3, ask: *What do Jake's actions tell you about him as a character?*

- **Word Work:** Introduce the term *apostrophe*. Remind students to place an apostrophe in place of the removed letter.

 Tier 3

- **Narrative Elements: Setting:** See the note for on-level learners.

- **Compare and Contrast:** For item 4, have students compare the actions of the pioneer kids to behavior of kids today in similar circumstances.

- **Draw Conclusions:** For item 3, ask: *What do Jake's actions tell you about him as a character?* Have them put themselves in Jake's position and tell what they would have done in the same situation.

- **Word Work:** Ask students to share what they know about contractions and examples of words with apostrophes. If appropriate, give examples of apostrophes inserted to replace more than one letter, as in words like *you'd, he'd,* and *who'd.*

Skills:
- Understanding narrative elements
- Drawing conclusions
- Comparing and contrasting

Teacher Boy:
Reading Passage

© The Granger Collection

    Jake and Emma followed the creek. Then they turned up the hill on the mining road to get to the school. It was more than a mile to walk. Jake carried their lunches in a cloth bag. The bag also held an almanac. That was the only book Jake had.

    It was Emma's first year of schooling. She was eight. Jake was twelve. He started school three years back. School was not the most important thing for pioneer kids like Jake and Emma. First came chores. Some kids milked cows and goats. Others hauled water, baked bread, or built fences. Jake got up before dawn. His job was to sweep his dad's dry-goods store.

    Soon the schoolhouse came into view. It wasn't fancy. It was just a small wooden building. But it was new and clean. It had a plank floor and benches to sit on. A wood stove kept away the chill. A single window let in some light. A water bucket hung in a corner. Everybody shared its tin dipper when they got thirsty.

(continued)

Teacher Boy: Reading Passage

(continued)

It was Jake who first noticed something was wrong. He didn't hear the iron school bell's clang. He didn't see Miss Colter. His ten classmates waited outside. There was nobody to invite them in.

Jake knew that school had to start. He took charge. He called the kids inside. He asked Seth to fill the bucket. He told the others to sit and take out any books they had.

The students were as young as six and as old as fifteen. Clay was thirteen, and was just starting school. Emma knew all her letters, so she offered to teach Clay. Jake asked Sara to lead writing practice. He and three others did math. They chanted, "8 times 6 is 48. 8 times 7 is 56."

But Jake wasn't a real teacher, so some kids acted up. Some started wrestling. Others threw pebbles. They were so much better behaved for Miss Colter. They respected her. She was a lady.

Jake was about to give up when he heard a wagon. Everyone else heard it, too. They quickly settled down. Miss Colter had arrived at last!

"My, you're all being so good!" she chirped as she entered. "I'm sorry I'm late," she said. "My horse went lame and couldn't pull my wagon. So I walked down to see my nearest neighbor. He brought me here. Better late than never!"

Miss Colter untied her bonnet and hung it on a nail. "Now, class," she said, smiling. "Let's have our spelling bee!"

Name _____   Date _____

 # Teacher Boy: Activity Sheet

(Read and Understand) Read the passage. Then answer these questions.

1. This story takes place long ago. Circle two clues that show this.

2. Read the third paragraph. How is this school different from your school?

_____

_____

3. What was wrong at school that morning? _____

4. Why did the students behave well for Miss Colter? _____

_____

(Word Work: Contractions)

Read the words. Write the contraction.

Words	Contraction
did not	
you are	
it is	
is not	

 ## Tip

Contractions are formed by combining two words into one. We leave out letters. We fill the space with an *apostrophe*.

Examples:

was not = **wasn't** — the *o* is taken out

I am = **I'm** — the *a* is taken out

Wasn't and I'm are **contractions**.

(Check) Circle the best choice.

Why was school not the most important thing for pioneer children?

A. They already knew how to read.

B. They had no way to get to school.

C. Chores came first.

D. Books were not made then.

Name _____ Date _____

 # Teacher Boy: Activity Sheet

Read and Understand) Read the passage. Then answer these questions.

1. This story takes place long ago. Circle three clues that show this.

2. How was the pioneer school different from yours? Write three ways that it was

different. _____

_____

3. What did Jake do to help when something was wrong, and why did he do it?

_____

4. Why did the students behave well for Miss Colter? _____

_____

Word Work: Contractions

Read each contraction. Write the two separate words.

Contraction	Words
doesn't	
you're	
it's	
haven't	

 Tip

Contractions are formed by combining two words into one. We leave out letters. We fill the space with an *apostrophe*.

Examples:

was not = **wasn't** — the *o* is taken out

I am = **I'm** — the *a* is taken out

Wasn't and I'm are **contractions**.

Check) Circle the best choice.

Why was school not the most important for thing pioneer children?

A. They already knew how to read.

B. They had no way to get to school.

C. Chores came first.

D. Books were not made then.

Differentiated Activities for Teaching Key Comprehension Skills: Grades 2–3 © 2010 by Martin Lee and Marcia Miller. Scholastic Teaching Resources

Name _____ Date _____

 # Teacher Boy: Activity Sheet

Read and Understand Read the passage. Then answer these questions.

1. What tells you that this story does not take place today? Circle three clues.

2. What are three ways to compare your school to the school in the passage?

_____

3. What problem did Jake face when he got to school and how did he try to solve it?

_____

_____

4. Tell what happened when Miss Colter arrived and how you think the children felt.

_____

_____

Word Work: Contractions

Read each sentence. Find two words you can make into one.
Circle the two words. Then write the contraction in the next column.

Sentence	Contraction
You are going to be late.	
We are having a spelling bee.	
It is the coldest day of the week.	
The kids did not behave well for Jake.	

 Tip

Contractions are formed by combining two words into one. We leave out letters. We fill the space with an *apostrophe*.

Example:

was not = **wasn't**

I am = **I'm**

Check Circle the best choice.

What did you learn about pioneer schools from "Teacher Boy"?

A. The teachers were always late.

B. All children walked a long way to school.

C. Classes had students of all ages and levels.

D. They had lots of books and materials.

Teaching **Rascal of the Ranch**

Skills:
- Determining author's purpose
- Recognizing cause and effect
- Analyzing text structure

Students read a biographical sketch about a remarkable dog and his owner.

Tasks	Tier 1 Below Level	Tier 2 On Level	Tier 3 Above Level
Determine the author's purpose		X	X
Recognize cause-and-effect relationships	X	X	X
Identify direct quotations	X	X	X
Gather information from a title	X	X	X
Use variant spellings of the /oo/ sound	X	X	X
Generate rhyming words			X

Getting Started

See the tips below for introducing the lesson. Make copies of the reading passage (pages 33–34) and the appropriate leveled activity sheet for each group of learners (pages 35–37).

Access prior knowledge by discussing what students know about teaching tricks to a dog, as well as how to use punctuation marks with direct quotations. Build background on ranch life and rodeos.

◆ Tier 1

- **Text Structure:** Read aloud the title and discuss its meaning before students respond to item 1. Review that quotation marks always come in pairs to form brackets or the "bread" of a "sandwich" around the exact words that someone says. Invite students to take turns saying those words as David might say them.

- **Cause and Effect:** To answer items 3 and 4, ask students to locate the paragraphs in which the details are given so they can support their responses.

- **Word Work:** Brainstorm with students other words that have the /o͞o/ sound. List and sort the words by how the /o͞o/ sound is spelled. Include proper names, such as Sue or Lewis.

● Tier 2

- **Text Structure:** Discuss the title and its meaning. Invite students to suggest rascal-like behaviors that a dog might display. Compare and contrast the concepts of a ranch and a farm. Then have students answer items 1 and 2. Ask them to find other direct quotations.

- **Cause and Effect:** To answer item 3, ask students to locate the evidence found in the text to support their responses. Clarify that very few dogs learn tricks as quickly and easily as Skidboot did.

- **Author's Purpose:** Before students answer item 4, clarify that an author may have multiple reasons for writing a biography. Discuss different motivations.

- **Word Work:** Extend by having students use the remaining three words in original sentences related to the selection.

⬠ Tier 3

- **Author's Purpose:** For item 1, discuss the purposes authors have for writing different styles of text. Have students recall a biography they have read and why they think the author wrote it.

- **Cause and Effect:** To answer item 2, have students find support for their responses. Ask other cause-effect questions about the story, such as: *Why did Skidboot get $25,000?* or *Why did David nearly give Skidboot away?*

- **Text Structure:** Review the use of quotation marks around the exact words a speaker says. Invite students to speculate how the author might have obtained that quotation. Have them suggest other hard work people do because they like it. Then have them answer item 3.

- **Word Work:** Encourage students to use a dictionary to help them confirm spellings.

Skills:
- Determining author's purpose
- Recognizing cause and effect
- Analyzing text structure

Rascal of the Ranch:
Reading Passage

courtesy of www.skidboot.com

David Hartwig is a rancher in Texas. He trains and shoes horses. He works hard and keeps busy. "It's not hard work if you enjoy it," he says.

Life changed for David on Christmas Eve, 1992. He'd been too busy to get his wife a gift. His last job was to shoe horses for a friend, and that friend let him have a puppy for his wife. It seemed like a good gift. David picked a lively pup and named him Skidboot.

What kind of name is that? A skidboot is a strong leather boot. Rodeo horses wear them to protect their back legs. A skidboot is tough—just like that pup.

Skidboot was smart and curious, but he always got into trouble. What a rascal! It got so bad that David almost gave Skidboot away. Still, that dog was special. Skidboot watched closely and copied what he saw. If a horse limped, Skidboot limped. If David rolled over, he rolled over. David got an idea. He would teach Skidboot tricks. Maybe that would calm the rascal.

Skidboot's first trick was "Whoa!" David taught Skidboot that "whoa!" means stop. Could Skidboot learn it if David showed him? Skidboot watched David. He learned "Whoa" after three tries. David would say "Whoa!" and Skidboot would stop and stand still.

(continued)

Rascal of the Ranch: Reading Passage

(continued)

Next, Skidboot learned "Get it." He got it very quickly. Then he learned "Back up." Could Skidboot become a ranch helper? David tested him. He let a calf loose and called "Get it." Skidboot ran toward the calf. When he was almost there, David called, "Whoa!" Skidboot froze. Then David said, "Back up." His smart dog did just that.

courtesy of www.skidboot.com

David taught Skidboot many tricks, like "Play dead," "Crawl," "Bow," and "Pull." Soon Skidboot and David did tricks at rodeos. People loved seeing them in action.

Skidboot and David were a hit at the Texas State Fair. That dog became a star! He won $25,000 on a TV pet contest. He performed on famous talk shows. He visited schools and hospitals. Was Skidboot the smartest dog ever?

Skidboot lived a happy life. He and David stayed best pals until the end. Skidboot closed his eyes for the last time in 2007. He was fourteen years old. That's a long life for a big dog. David buried him on his ranch near an oak tree.

David still trains and shoes horses. He has other dogs. But there will never be another Skidboot!

Rascal of the Ranch: Activity Sheet

Read and Understand) Read the passage. Then answer these questions.

1. Underline the title. What does it tell about Skidboot? _____

2. What are the exact words David said about being busy? Circle them.

3. Why did David get a pup that Christmas Eve? _____

_____

4. What made Skidboot famous? _____

_____

Word Work: The /o͞o/ Sound

The letters *oo* in Skid<u>boo</u>t make the /o͞o/ sound. Other letters make that sound, too.

Read the words in the box. Then say each one out loud.
Circle five words that have an /o͞o/ sound.

blue	oak	shoe	whoa
bow	school	who	you

Check) Circle the best choice.

What word did David say to make Skidboot stop?

A. "Crawl!"

B. "Pull!"

C. "Sit!"

D. "Whoa!"

Rascal of the Ranch: Activity Sheet

Read and Understand Read the passage. Then answer these questions.

1. After you read the title, what did you expect the passage to be about? _____

_____

2. What exact words did David say that tell how he felt about his job? _____

3. How did Skidboot learn tricks so fast? _____

4. Why do you think the author wrote this story? _____

Word Work: The /ōō/ Sound

The letters *oo* in Skidb<u>oo</u>t make the /ōō/ sound.
Other letters make the /ōō/ sound, too.

Write each /ōō/ word from the box in a sentence below.

bow
hoop
knew
oak
school
shoe
true
whoa

David _____ that Skidboot was a special dog.

A biography is a _____ story of someone's life.

David and Skidboot performed at a _____.

David fit his horse with a brand new _____.

Skidboot learned to jump through a _____.

Check Circle the best choice.

Why did David decide to teach Skidboot tricks?

A. to become famous

B. to try to calm Skidboot

C. to test how smart the dog was

D. to help him train horses

Rascal of the Ranch: Activity Sheet

Read and Understand) Read the passage. Then answer these questions.

1. Why do you think the author wrote this story? Give two reasons.

_____

_____

2. How did Skidboot act like a rascal? _____

_____

3. What exact words did David say to show that he liked his job? _____

_____

Word Work: The /o͞o/ Sound)

Read each word with the /o͞o/ sound as in Skidb<u>oo</u>t. Circle the letters that make the /o͞o/ sound. Then write three rhyming words that spell /o͞o/ the same way.

Word with /o͞o/ sound	Rhyming Words Spelled the Same Way
too	
blue	
flew	
room	

Check) Circle the best choice.

Why did David decide to teach Skidboot tricks?

A. to become famous

B. to try to calm Skidboot

C. to test how smart the dog was

D. to help him train horses

Teaching **The Giant Hairy Toe**

Students read a mid-Atlantic American folktale.

Skills:

- Identifying narrative elements
- Recognizing cause-and-effect relationships
- Exploring folktale as a genre

Tasks	Tier 1 Below Level	Tier 2 On Level	Tier 3 Above Level
Identify narrative elements (characters, setting, plot)	X	X	X
Recognize cause-and-effect relationships	X	X	X
Explore genre: folktale		X	X
Use irregular verbs	X	X	
Use compound words			X

Getting Started

See the tips below for introducing the lesson. Make copies of the reading passage (pages 39–40) and the appropriate leveled activity sheet for each group of learners (pages 41–43).

Access prior knowledge by recalling folktales students know and discussing oral tradition. Also review aspects of pioneer life.

◆ Tier 1

- **Identify Narrative Elements:** Talk about the three building blocks of a story: *characters* (who it's about), *setting* (time and place), and *plot* (what happens). Then answer items 1 and 2 together, highlighting each narrative element.

- **Develop Vocabulary:** Ask children to act out *huddling,* and give an example of when they might huddle.

- **Cause and Effect:** Answer item 3 together, inviting children to give other examples of cause and effect in the story.

- **Word Work:** As needed, review *verb tense* (past vs. present). Have children locate past-tense verbs in the passage that have *–ed*, such as *growled, licked*, and *wrapped*. You might have struggling writers use a highlighter to find examples in the text instead of copying them.

● Tier 2

- **Identify Narrative Elements:** Review narrative elements as the building blocks of a story: *characters* (who it's about), *setting* (time and place), and *plot* (what happens). Then have children answer items 1 and 2 on their own. Encourage them to share their responses to item 5.

- **Develop Vocabulary:** Have children pretend to be the old woman as she *froze*.

- **Cause and Effect:** Discuss students' responses to item 4, and review cause-and-effect relationships between characters' actions.

- **Word Work:** Have children locate verbs that have a *–d* added to signal past tense, as in *lived, tasted*, and *rumbled*. Allow weaker writers to shorten the example sentences to include only the subject and verb. Point out *froze* as an example of an irregular verb in past tense.

⬠ Tier 3

- **Identify Narrative Elements:** Encourage children to think about characters, setting, and plot. as they answer items 1–4.

- **Cause and Effect:** Ask students to describe the cause-and-effect relationships in the passage when they discuss the events of the woman finding the toe, then eating it and the giant returning, then the woman disappearing.

- **Develop Vocabulary:** Relate *hollow* objects, such as tubes or pipes, to hollow voices. Explain that hollow objects have physical emptiness, while hollow voices have emotional emptiness.

- **Word Work:** Brainstorm with children other compound words, such as *chalkboard, laptop*, and *playground*. Challenge them to rephrase parts of the story using compound words. For example, *woodland creatures* could replace "creatures of the woods."

Name _____ Date _____

Skills:
- Identifying narrative elements
- Recognizing cause-and-effect relationships
- Exploring folktale as a genre

(A Folktale From Maryland)

The Giant Hairy Toe:
Reading Passage

Once upon a time, a poor old woman lived alone in a tiny hut deep in the woods. One day, the woman went to her vegetable patch to pick ingredients for soup. She saw an odd lump by the fence. She bent down to have a closer look. It was a huge hairy toe!

It had been weeks since the woman had tasted meat. Her stomach growled as she licked her lips. "Mmm! Meat!"

She took the giant toe back to her hut and cooked up a steaming kettle of hairy toe soup. How great it tasted! The old woman ate three bowls of it. She went to bed in jolly spirits. Her belly was full at last. Soon she was asleep.

At about midnight, wild winds suddenly kicked up. There were moaning noises around the hut. Thick clouds blocked out every drop of moonlight.

A deep voice rumbled, "Hairy toe! Hairy toe! Who took my hairy toe?" The old woman stirred in her sleep while the creatures of the woods went on alert. Field mice hid in their holes. Foxes kept quiet under their bushy tails. Bears huddled deep inside their dark dens.

(continued)

The Giant Hairy Toe: Reading Passage

(continued)

Stomp, stomp! A hollow voice called, "Hairy toe! Hairy toe! Who took my hairy toe?" This time, the old woman woke up. She wrapped her quilt tightly around herself. She held her pillow over her ears.

The stomping grew louder still as it approached the hut. That hollow voice kept calling, "Hairy toe! Hairy toe! Who took my hairy toe?" The old woman glanced at the soup pot. She began to quiver.

Then the stomping crashed through the garden fence. Up sat the old woman, her eyes wide open. She was terrified now. She rushed barefoot to the door and closed the thick iron bolt. She dragged a heavy table to block the entrance. Back in bed, she shivered and waited.

Crack! The bolt snapped off. The door burst open. The table flew across the room and splintered apart. A soup bowl shattered on the floor. The stomping made the narrow bed wobble and the floorboards groan.

The old woman froze. It was an unbelievable sight. A monstrous giant stood in her hut. He stared down at her, breathing hard. His hollow voice snarled, "Hairy toe! Hairy toe! Who took my hairy toe?"

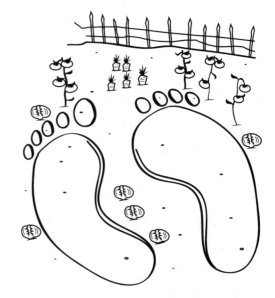

The woman jumped up, trying to look tall and brave. She screamed, "*I* took your hairy toe. *I* cooked your hairy toe. And then *I ATE* it!"

The giant smiled. "Yes," he said softly. "I know you did."

Nobody ever saw the old woman again. But neighbors spotted huge footprints in her garden. Nobody noticed that the right footprint had only four toes.

The Giant Hairy Toe: Activity Sheet

(**Read and Understand**) Read the passage. Then answer these questions.

1. Who are the main characters? _____

On the back of this page, draw a picture of each character.

2. Where does the story take place? _____

Do you know when it takes place? _____

3. Why was the old woman so happy at bedtime? Circle the part that describes this.

4. How would bears *huddle*? Why would they do this? _____

_____

(**Word Work: Irregular Verbs**)

Some verbs use *–ed* to show action in the past
PRESENT: Today I <u>walk</u>.   **PAST:** Last week I <u>walked</u>.

Other verbs have new spellings to show action in the past.
PRESENT: Today I <u>run</u>.   **PAST:** Last week I <u>ran</u>.

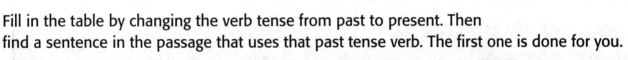

Fill in the table by changing the verb tense from past to present. Then
find a sentence in the passage that uses that past tense verb. The first one is done for you.

Verb in the PRESENT	Verb in the PAST	Find the sentence. Copy it here.
is	was	Her belly **was** full at last.
go	<u>w</u> __ __ __	
see	<u>s</u> __ __	
eat	<u>a</u> __ __	

(**Check**) Circle the best choice.

Why did the old woman wake up in the middle of the night?

A. She needed an extra blanket.   C. She was very hungry.

B. She heard scary noises.   D. Her door burst open.

The Giant Hairy Toe: Activity Sheet

Read and Understand Read the passage. Then answer these questions.

1. Where does the story take place? When do you think it happened? _____

_____

2. What is it meant by saying that the old woman froze? _____

3. Why did the giant visit the hut? _____

4. What do you think happened to the old woman? _____

Word Work: Irregular Verbs

Some verbs use –ed to show action in the past.
PRESENT: Today I <u>walk</u>.   **PAST:** Last week I <u>walked</u>.

Other verbs have new spellings to show action in the past.
PRESENT: Today I <u>run</u>.   **PAST:** Last week I <u>ran</u>.

Fill in the table below. First underline the verb that shows action in the past. Then rewrite the sentence. Use the same verb to show action now. The first one is done for you.

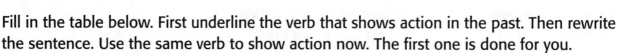

Sentence With Past-Tense Verbs	Sentence With Present-Tense Verbs
She <u>saw</u> an odd lump by the fence.	She <u>sees</u> an odd lump by the fence.
She bent down for a closer look.	
So she took the hairy toe back to her hut.	
She held her pillow over her ears.	

Check Circle the best choice.

Which is the best clue that something scary will happen?

A. The old woman lived in the woods.   C. Bears were in their dens.

B. The old woman ate three bowls of soup.   D. The bolt snapped off the door.

Differentiated Activities for Teaching Key Comprehension Skills: Grades 2–3 © 2010 by Martin Lee and Marcia Miller. Scholastic Teaching Resources

The Giant Hairy Toe: Activity Sheet

(Read and Understand) Read the passage. Then answer these questions.

1. Why do you think the setting works well for this kind of story? _____

_____

2. Why did the old woman eat the toe? _____

3. Circle three scary parts in the story. Why do these parts hold your interest?

_____

4. What other words could describe a hollow voice? _____

(Word Work: Compound Words)

A *compound* word is made of two separate words put together as one.
Grandfather comes from **grand + father**. It means a father's father.
Find five compound words in the story and fill in the chart. The first one is done for you.

Compound Word	Separate Words	Meaning
moonlight	moon + light	light from the moon
	+	
	+	
	+	

(Check) Circle the best choice.

What proof is there that the angry giant came to the tiny hut?

A. There was a broken soup bowl on the floor.

B. Animals in the nearby woods took cover.

C. The huge footprint in the garden had only four toes.

D. The woman found a hairy toe in her garden.

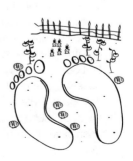

Teaching **The Echidna: An Odd Mammal**

Students read an informational science text.

Tasks	Tier 1 Below Level	Tier 2 On Level	Tier 3 Above Level
Set a purpose for reading nonfiction	X	X	X
Use text organizers (bulleted lists, italics, parentheses)	X	X	X
Compare and contrast		X	X
Use the possessive ending -'s	X	X	
Use the superlative ending -est			X

Getting Started

See the tips below for introducing the lesson. Make copies of the reading passage (pages 45–46) and the appropriate leveled activity sheet for each group of learners (pages 47–49).

Access prior knowledge and build background on mammals and Australia's habitats. Review text organizers such as bulleted lists, italics, pronunciations, and parentheses.

◆ Tier 1

- **Set a Purpose for Reading:** Discuss how setting a purpose for reading helps readers predict what the passage is about, guides reading, and makes reading interactive. The title, illustrations, and text organizers can provide clues. Answer item 1 together.

- **Use Text Organizers:** Introduce the term *bulleted list*. Make bulleted lists together that support a topic sentence. Then answer item 2 together. Extend by posing a similar question about paragraph 4.

- **Word Work:** Identify the *apostrophe* as a punctuation mark that looks like a comma, but is placed higher in relation to the words on the line. Make up possessive phrases using children's names, such as "a book that belongs to Roy" and write the possessive form ("Roy's book") on the board. Invite volunteers to insert the apostrophe where it belongs. Then have children complete the table.

● Tier 2

- **Set a Purpose for Reading:** Talk about ways to set a purpose for reading, such as using a title and illustrations to build interest, or asking questions to guide reading. Then invite children to suggest various responses to item 1.

- **Use Text Organizers:** Examine the pronunciation given in parentheses in paragraph 3 and the use of italicized text. Then have children answer item 2.

- **Compare and Contrast:** Review *comparing* as finding common features, and *contrasting* as finding opposing features. After children have answered items 3 and 4, have them share their responses to provide an additional opportunity to compare and contrast.

- **Word Work:** Review the *apostrophe* and its use to signal the possessive form. Invite volunteers to make up and write possessive phrases about classmates. Then have children complete the table.

⬠ Tier 3

- **Set a Purpose for Reading:** Have children make a K-W-L chart for echidnas, working on the What We Know and What We Want to Know columns before reading and completing the What We Learned column after reading. Then have them answer items 1 and 2 independently.

- **Compare and Contrast:** Consider having students work in pairs to answer items 3 and 4.

- **Word Work:** Invite children to share the sentences they created. Extend by suggesting words whose spelling changes when –*est* ending is added, such as *clumsy (clumsiest)* or *thin (thinnest)*.

Skills:
- Setting a purpose for reading nonfiction
- Using text organizers
- Comparing and contrasting

The Echidna: An Odd Mammal:
Reading Passage

Have you ever thought about what animal group you belong to? Scientists organize animals into groups that share main features, such as having hair or fur. One important group of animals is *mammals*. Mammals come in many sizes and shapes. Dogs, mice, lions, bats, whales, rabbits, and humans are just some of the mammals you know. Scientists count more than 5,000 kinds of mammals in the world!

All mammals share key features. Here are some of them:

- Mammals have backbones.

- Mammals are warm-blooded. (Their body temperature stays about the same all year.)

- Mammals have hair or fur. (A porcupine is a mammal. Its quills are stiff hairs.)

- Mammal mothers give birth to live babies.

- Mammal mothers feed their babies with milk that their body produces.

And then there is the *echidna* (e-KID-na). This odd mammal lives in Australia. The echidna is also called the *spiny anteater*. Each spine is a stiff hair. The echidna has short legs. Its feet have long heavy claws, so it is clumsy when it walks. But it likes to swim.

(continued)

The Echidna: An Odd Mammal: Reading Passage

(continued)

The echidna is one of nature's oldest animals. Echidnas have been around since the days of the dinosaurs. Picture some of an echidna's surprising features:

- It has spines like a porcupine.

- It has a pouch like a kangaroo.

- It can live as long as an elephant.

- Its snout is like the beak of a bird.

- It lays leathery eggs like a snake. (The *platypus* is the only other mammal that lays eggs.)

Bugs are the echidna's favorite food. The echidna has a pointy snout. Its tongue is long and sticky. These features help it eat ants and termites. But the echidna has no teeth. It crushes its food with its strong tongue.

Echidnas are quiet and shy. The only sound they make is sniffing. A scared echidna curls up into a spiky ball. Or it quickly digs straight down into the ground to hide.

Baby echidnas are called *puggles*. First the mother echidna lays an egg. This egg is smaller than a jelly bean. The egg grows inside a pouch on the mother's belly. Soon the puggle hatches. It feeds on its mother's milk. It lives in her pouch until its spines and claws grow. Then it enters the outside world.

What an odd mammal!

 Differentiated Activities for Teaching Key Comprehension Skills: Grades 2–3 © 2010 by Martin Lee and Marcia Miller. Scholastic Teaching Resources

The Echidna: Activity Sheet

Read and Understand Read the passage. Then answer these questions.

1. Circle the title. What does it make you want to know? _____

_____

2. Draw a box around paragraph 2. It gives five facts in a list.
Circle two sentences that come *before* the list that tell why the facts go together.

3. Where in the world do echidnas live? _____

4. What is a puggle? _____

Why does that word appear in *italics*? _____

Word Work: Possessive Ending –'s

In the passage, find three words that end with –'s.
Write each word beside its meaning.

Possessive Meaning	Word Ending With –'s
is part of the mother	
belongs to an echidna	
is part of nature	

 Tip

When a noun ends in –'s, the word after it "belongs to" it or "is part of" it.

Example:

the girl's book
(the book that belongs to the girl)

Check Circle the best choice.

What can the echidna do that only one other mammal in the world can do?

A. curl up into a ball   C. eat without teeth

B. feed milk to its baby   D. lay eggs

● The Echidna: Activity Sheet

Read and Understand Read the passage. Then answer these questions.

1. What do you want to find out by reading this passage? _____

_____

2. The dots in front of items in a list are called *bullets*. Look at the second list of sentences with bullets. Circle the sentence that tells why they go together.

3. In what ways is the echidna like a dog? _____

_____

4. List three reasons why the echidna is such an odd mammal._____

_____

_____

Word Work: Possessive Ending –'s

In the passage, find three words that end with –'s.
Copy them into the table. Then write what each word means.

Word Ending With –'s	What It Means
	is part of _____
	belongs to the _____
	is part of the _____

 Tip

An –'s at the end of a noun means that the word after it "belongs to" it or "is part of" it.

Example:

in Australia's desert *(the desert that is part of Australia)*

Check Circle the best choice.

In which way is an echidna unlike a porcupine?

A. The echidna is warm-blooded.

B. The echidna has sharp spines.

C. The echidna is a mammal.

D. The echidna lays eggs.

The Echidna: Activity Sheet

Read and Understand Read the passage. Then answer these questions.

1. What question about echidnas could you ask to help guide your reading? _____

_____

2. Circle three sentences that appear inside parentheses (___).

Why are these marks used? _____

3. Why does the author compare the echidna with five different animals? _____

_____

4. The author compares the echidna's snout to a bird's beak. How else is an echidna like and unlike a bird?

_____

Word Work: Superlative Ending *–est*

Add *–est* to the end of each word in the table.
Tell what the new word means.
Then write a short sentence for each *–est* word.

 Tip

The ending *–est* is used to compare three or more things.

Word	+ *–est*	Meaning	Use the Word in a Sentence
old	oldest	older than all the rest	The echidna is one of the oldest animals on Earth.
strong			
small			
warm			

Check Circle the best choice.

Why is the echidna a clumsy walker?

A. Its snout is so thin and pointy.

B. Its stubby legs have long claws.

C. It walks like a dinosaur.

D. It usually swims.

Teaching **Goal!**

Students read a play set after a children's soccer game.

Tasks	Tier 1 Below Level	Tier 2 On Level	Tier 3 Above Level
Understand setting and characters in a play	X	X	X
Identify text structures in a script	X	X	X
Use text elements to enhance comprehension	X	X	X
Make inferences	X	X	X
Recognize and distinguish between homophones	X	X	X

Getting Started

See the tips below for introducing the lesson. Make copies of the reading passage (pages 51–52) and the appropriate leveled activity sheet for each group of learners (pages 53–55).

Access prior knowledge about plays. Build background on text conventions used in scripts. Review homophones.

Tier 1

- **Text Structure:** Compare and contrast a play with a story. Point out key parts of a script: character list; setting; names of speakers and their lines; stage directions. Then read the play with the group. Stop to ask and answer questions as needed. Have students answer items 1 and 2.

- **Make Inferences:** Pose questions that are not stated directly, such as: *Why is Lia almost in tears? How does Mom try to cheer Lia up?*

- **Narrative Elements:** Guide students to locate the text evidence they need to answer items 3 and 4.

- **Word Work:** Talk about why homophones can be tricky. Encourage students to practice recalling key homophones, such as *to/too/two*, *know/no*, and *wear/where*. Work on this activity together. Extend by exploring other common homophones.

Tier 2

- **Text Structure:** Ask students what they know about how the script for a play is written. Discuss how it compares to the way text is structured in a story. Read the play as a group. Have students complete items 1 and 2.

- **Make Inferences:** Pose questions not stated directly, such as: *Why does Lia listen to Nate rather than to her mom? How would Tim know that "Nate can always eat"?*

- **Narrative Elements:** Guide students to identify evidence in the play to answer items 3 and 4. Ask: *Why aren't Hannah and her coach listed as characters? (They have no lines to say.)*

- **Word Work:** Explain that the many homophones in English can make comprehension tricky. Help students recall and use common ones, such as *to/too/two*, *know/no*, and *there/their/they're*. List other homophones students know.

Tier 3

- **Text Structures:** With students' input, create a Venn diagram to compare and contrast plays and stories. Talk about what structures students notice when they skim the reading passage. After reading the play together, have students complete items 1 and 2. Extend by discussing: *Why doesn't every line include a stage direction?*

- **Make Inferences:** Challenge students to think about the play as an actor or director might. For example: *How should the characters sit? Should Lia seem angry or sad? Why is Mom so patient?*

- **Narrative Elements:** Before students answer items 3 and 4, ask why a play includes a setting. *(There is little or no description in the dialogue.)*

- **Word Work:** Have students complete this activity in pairs.

Skills:

- Using text structure to comprehend a play

- Understanding narrative elements: characters and setting

- Making inferences

Goal!
Reading Passage

Characters:

    Mom

    Tim, *boy of 10, brother to Lia*

    Lia, *girl of 8, a soccer player and sister to Tim*

    Nate, *boy of 8, member of another soccer team, friend to Lia and Tim*

Setting: *In the car, on the way home after a soccer game*

TIM: That was a great game, Lia. You were terrific!

MOM: Yes, you gave it your best effort! I'm so proud of you!

LIA: *[nearly in tears]* I'm not proud. I'm miserable. We lost.

MOM: It was a close game, Lia. Everyone played so well.

LIA: Not me. I didn't even score a goal. I stink.

MOM: Nobody on your team scored, honey. And the Lemons scored only one goal.

NATE: Hannah scored our goal. She scores most of our goals.

TIM: Hannah can really play well. She's sure fast, too.

MOM: *[calmly]* The last time you played the Lemons, they got four goals. Remember, Lia? So your team is getting better. And you'll play the Lemons one more time.

LIA: We lost, Mom. You saw. Losing isn't getting better. Losing is just losing.

(continued)

Goal! Reading Passage

(continued)

TIM: Come on, Lia. You don't get it.

MOM: The Lemons are a very good team. What's important is that you had a good time. You played hard. You played fair. And you tried your best. Tim and I had lots of fun watching you and cheering you on.

LIA: Well, I didn't have lots of fun.

TIM: Lia, you can't win every game. I think you're just having a bad day.

NATE: *[quietly]* I don't think you stink, Lia.

LIA: *[after a pause]* You don't?

NATE: No. And our coach doesn't think so, either.

LIA: She doesn't?

NATE: No, she doesn't.

LIA: How do you know that? I didn't score. I didn't even come close.

NATE: That's because we tried so hard to stop you. Coach said, "Watch out for number 7. She's a good player. Keep the ball away from her."

LIA: She said that? About me?

NATE: She said that. About you.

TIM: See! I told you that you don't stink.

LIA: *[smiling]* Okay. But I *do* need some food. I'm starving!

TIM: Me, too. And Nate can always eat!

NATE   That's true!

MOM: Let's go for pizza. How's that for a goal, kids?

LIA: *[really smiling!]* It sounds terrific. That's the kind of goal I like.

MOM: That's my girl!

LIA: When do we play your team again, Nate? I owe you a goal!

TIM: That's my little sister!

Name _____ Date _____

 # Goal! Activity Sheet

Read and Understand) **Read the passage. Then answer these questions.**

1. Who are the characters in the play? Circle each of their names.

2. Underline the words that tell where the play is set.
Draw a box around the words that tell when the play is set.

3. What is the name of the team that beat Lia's team? _____

4. How did Nate help Lia feel better? _____

_____

Word Work: Homophones)

Look at the boxes below. Draw a line to match
each homophone to its meaning.

hour	60 minutes
our	belongs to us
pause	an animal's feet
paws	stop for a moment

 ## Tip

Homophones are words that
sound alike but have different
spellings and different meanings.

Example:

won and *one*

One is a number.
Won means came first in a
game or contest

Check) Circle the best choice.

Which character played on the winning soccer team?

A. Mom   C. Lia

B. Tim   D. Nate

Name _____   Date _____

 Goal! Activity Sheet

(Read and Understand) Read the passage. Then answer these questions.

1. Why is there a list of names in uppercase letters on the left side of the page? _____

_____

2. Where and when is this scene taking place? _____

_____

3. Who played for the Lemons? Circle two clues that tell.

4. Who is Hannah? _____

Why do Nate and Tim talk about her? _____

(Word Work: Homophones)

Read the sentences below. Circle two homophones in each.

The new iron grate looks great!

Two hours is too long to wait!

Do you know why we have no recess?

Is it fair for kids to pay full bus fare?

 Tip

Homophones are words that sound alike but have different spellings and different meanings.

Example:

meet and *meat*
Let's *meet* the cook who grilled this tasty *meat*!

(Check) Circle the best choice.

Which two characters are in the same family?

A. Mom and Nate

B. Tim and Nate

C. Lia and Tim

D. Nate and Lia

Differentiated Activities for Teaching Key Comprehension Skills: Grades 2–3 © 2010 by Martin Lee and Marcia Miller. Scholastic Teaching Resources

Name _____   Date _____

 # Goal! Activity Sheet

Read and Understand Read the passage. Then answer these questions.

1. Why isn't there text in the play such as "he said" and "she said"? _____

_____

2. Why are some words in brackets, such as "[nearly in tears]"? _____

_____

3. Where and when does the play take place? _____

_____

4. Why does Mom think that Lia's team is getting better? _____

_____

Word Work: Homophones

Find a homophone in the play for each word below.

Word	Homophone from the Play
grate	
teem	
no	
fare	
knot	

 Tip

Homophones are words that sound alike but have different spellings and different meanings.

Example:

Won and *one* are homophones. Read them in this sentence:

Nate's team *won* by only *one* goal.

Check Circle the best choice.

What number was on Lia's team shirt?

A. 1   B. 4   C. 7   D. 8

Teaching **Amber**

Skills:
- Setting purpose for reading
- Identifying main idea and details
- Drawing conclusions

Students read an article about an unusual gemstone.

Tasks	Tier 1 Below Level	Tier 2 On Level	Tier 3 Above Level
Set a purpose for reading nonfiction	X	X	X
Identify main idea and supporting details	X	X	X
Draw conclusions	X	X	X
Use context clues	X	X	X

Getting Started

See the tips below for introducing the lesson. Make copies of the reading passage (pages 57–58) and the appropriate leveled activity sheet for each group of learners (pages 59–61).

Access prior knowledge on informational articles and where they appear. Build background on fossils and the concept of extinction. Discuss different kinds of rocks, minerals, and gemstones.

◆ Tier 1

- **Set a Purpose for Reading:** Before they read the passages, help students predict what the passage is about or why it will be of interest. Display something amber in color to help students make the connection to the text. Have them read the title and discuss what they think they will learn from this piece.

- **Main Idea and Details:** Help students find the topic sentence in paragraph 3. Model how each sentence that follows gives a supporting detail. Then have students answer item 1. Repeat this procedure for paragraph 7 to enable students to answer item 2.

- **Draw Conclusions:** Talk about this description to help students draw conclusions about amber. To develop understanding, link each word with something students know. Help them answer item 3.

- **Word Work:** Consider pairing students to share their thinking as they seek clues to the meanings of the words in the box.

● Tier 2

- **Set a Purpose for Reading:** Before students read the passage, clarify that an informational article presents facts to readers to help them build understanding about the topic. Have students read the title and invite them to jot down questions they will keep in mind as they read.

- **Main Idea and Details:** Ask students to identify the topic sentence in paragraph 3, and then have them answer item 1. Repeat for paragraph 7, asking students to cite details that support their answer to item 2.

- **Draw Conclusions:** To help students answer item 3, brainstorm ideas and images evoked by the words *northern* and *gold*.

- **Word Work:** Model how to use context clues to understand the meanings of unfamiliar words.

⬠ Tier 3

- **Set a Purpose for Reading:** Some students may be inspired to learn more about amber. Before they read the passage, have them review the title and jot down questions that will guide them if they wish to do further research.

- **Main Idea and Details:** Have students read aloud the topic sentence in paragraph 3, and then use the supporting details to answer item 1.

- **Draw Conclusions:** Item 2 asks students to draw conclusions based on paragraph 7. Guide students to draw from the text, as well as their own knowledge. Invite volunteers to share their answers to item 3.

- **Word Work:** Challenge students to write sentences that include context clues in them.

Skills:
- Setting purpose for reading
- Identifying main idea and details
- Drawing conclusions

Amber:
Reading Passage

© topora/Shutterstock

Do you know the Amber Brown books? Amber is a clever character. Her hair is the color of her first name. Amber is both a girl's name and a color. But amber is much more!

Amber looks like a kind of gemstone. It is hard, like any stone. It is valuable, like many gems. Amber is worth far more a than plain stone. It is not, however, a stone.

Amber began as a sticky liquid called *resin*. It is found inside a plant. It feels like syrup. Fresh resin helps plants stay healthy. It can seal cracks if a branch breaks off. It fills in holes that animals chew or dig. Resin keeps out germs so a plant can heal.

Amber did not form the way stones have formed. Amber started out as the resin of ancient trees. It oozed out to protect them. Those ancient trees died out long ago, but the resin is still here. Air made it dry out and get hard. Over time, the resin turned into amber.

(continued)

Amber: Reading Passage

(continued)

People always valued amber for its warm honey color. They loved its smooth, hard, and glassy feel. Some called amber "frozen bits of sun." Others called it "northern gold." Maybe they thought it was a special kind of ice.

People have used amber in many ways. They have made it into bowls, jewelry, and charms. Some felt that amber had magic powers. They believed it could heal sick people or cure snake bites. To this day, amber is thought to bring good luck, long life, and peace. It is a birthstone for people born in November.

Scientists admire amber for other reasons. They study it to learn about life on earth long ago. Some of the finest amber has bits of extinct animals trapped in it. How did that happen? Maybe the creature landed on the resin by mistake and got stuck. If it couldn't get free, it died. Over time, more resin covered its body, drying it out and making a fossil that preserved, or saved, its shape. This is why fossils in amber show so many details. Amber fossils are tiny treasures. They let scientists peek at life forms from millions of years ago.

Amber is a beautiful gem. The best amber links the past with the present. One day you may see or hold some real amber. You may enjoy looking at its glowing color. How would you feel if you could hold a piece of the past in your hands?

© Galyna Andrushko/Shutterstock

Amber: Activity Sheet

Read and Understand Read the passage. Then answer these questions.

1. Circle the paragraph that tells about resin.

How does resin feel? _____

2. Underline the sentence that tells you why scientists study amber.

3. Why was amber called "frozen bits of sun"? _____

_____

Word Work: Context Clues

The following words come from the passage. Find and circle these four words in the text. Then look for clues to figure out the meaning of each word. Write the clues next to each.

Tip

Context clues are hints that help you figure out other words.

valuable _____

seals _____

cure _____

links _____

Check Circle the best choice.

Read the second paragraph on page 58.
What is the main idea of the paragraph?

A. Some felt that amber had magic powers.

B. They made it into bowls, jewelry, and charms.

C. People have used amber in many ways.

D. It is a birthstone for people born in November.

Name _____   Date _____

● Amber: Activity Sheet

(**Read and Understand**) Read the passage. Then answer these questions.

1. Circle the paragraph that tells about resin.

List three ways that resin helps a plant stay healthy. _____

_____

2. Why do scientists study amber? _____

_____

3. Why did some people call amber "northern gold"? _____

_____

(Word Work: Context Clues)

The following words come from the passage.
Find and circle these four words in the text.
Then write each word into the sentence where it fits.

valuable   seal   cure   links

The best _____ for the flu is lots of rest.

Gold is more _____ than paper.

The axle is a bar that _____ two wheels.

I used tape to _____ the gift box.

(Check) Circle the best choice.

How is amber different from other gems?

A. Amber is valuable.   C. Amber formed from plant resin.

B. Amber is hard.   D. Amber is a birthstone.

Amber: Activity Sheet

Read and Understand Read the passage. Then answer these questions.

1. Find the paragraph that describes resin.

List three details that tell how resin helps a plant stay healthy. _____

_____

2. Why is amber especially important to scientists? _____

_____

3. Answer the question the author asks at the end of "Amber."

_____

Word Work: Context Clues

The following words come from the passage. Find and circle these four words in the text. Then write a new sentence for each word.

Tip

Context clues are hints that help you figure out other words.

valuable _____

ancient _____

admire _____

birthstone _____

Check Circle the best choice.

Which statement is true only for the very finest amber?

A. It began as resin.

B. It is a kind of gemstone.

C. It has extinct matter trapped in it.

D. It is made into bowls, jewelry, and charms.

Teaching **Three Poems**

Students read a set of three poems about the month of March.

Skills:
- Exploring figurative language
- Identifying main idea and details
- Comparing and contrasting
- Analyzing an author's point of view

Tasks	Tier 1 Below Level	Tier 2 On Level	Tier 3 Above Level
Understand personification and metaphor	X	X	X
Identify main idea and supporting details	X	X	X
Compare and contrast	X	X	X
Identify synonyms	X	X	
Analyze an author's point of view			X
Identify antonyms			X
Examine rhyme scheme			X

Getting Started

See the tips below for introducing the lesson. Make copies of the reading passage (pages 63–64) and the appropriate leveled activity sheet for each group of learners (pages 65–67).

Access prior knowledge about the kinds of poems students have read. Review what it means for a poem to have end rhyme. Then discuss different forms of figurative language.

Tier 1

- **Main Idea:** Point out that each poem presents an image of a single idea. Help students look for similarities and differences among the poems, centered around the main idea. Then help them answer items 1 and 2.

- **Figurative Language:** Explain that poets often describe one thing in comparison to something else. Say: *We know that March is a month of the year. But two of the poets imagine March as a person who can do things.* Help students visualize each image as a way to help them answer items 3 and 4.

- **Word Work:** Discuss synonyms and why it helps writers to be able to use different words to express the same idea. Extend by having students brainstorm synonyms for other words in the poems.

Tier 2

- **Main Idea:** Clarify that each poem offers an image of one idea. Read the poems aloud chorally, or by alternating lines or verses. Ask students to search for similarities and differences among the poems. Then help them answer items 1 and 2.

- **Figurative Language:** Explain that a metaphor is a way to describe one thing as if it were something else. Say: *Poets know that March is a time of year, but they can imagine March as a person who does things.* Invite discussion about each image before assigning items 3 and 4.

- **Word Work:** Discuss why writers use synonyms instead of repeating the same words over and over. *(for variety, rhyme, clarity)* Invite students to use dictionaries as needed to complete this activity.

Tier 3

- **Main Idea:** Invite students to take turns reading the poems aloud individually or in groups. Ask them to compare and contrast each poet's image of March and then answer item 1.

- **Author's Point of View:** Challenge students to explain how each poet feels about March. Then have them answer item 2.

- **Figurative Language:** Talk about the saying, "March comes in like a lion and goes out like a lamb." Then have students answer item 3. For item 4, challenge students to explain why the poet mentions birds in her poem. *(to suggest the coming of spring)*

- **Word Work:** Relate synonyms and antonyms. Extend by brainstorming antonyms for other words that come up in reading materials or in classroom conversation.

Name _____ Date _____

Skills:
- Exploring figurative language
- Identifying main idea and details
- Comparing and contrasting
- Analyzing an author's point of view

Three Poems

March

by Mildred Pittinger

You're loud,
You're noisy,
    A blustery old chap!
You whistle,
You moan,
    You tear at my cap!
You blow,
You scowl,
    But, March, you are fair!
Part lion,
Part lamb,
    Now spring's in the air!

"March" by Mildred Pittinger is reprinted from POETRY PLACE ANTHOLOGY. Copyright © 1983 by Edgell Communications by permission of Scholastic Inc.

(continued)

Name _____ Date _____

Never Mind, March

Author Unknown

Never mind, March, we know
When you blow
You're not really mad
Or angry or bad;
You're only blowing the winter away
To get the world ready for April and May.

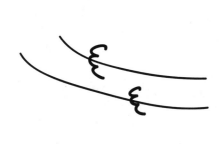

March

by Elizabeth Coatsworth

A blue day,
A blue jay
and a good beginning.
One crow,
melting snow—
spring's winning!

"March" by Elizabeth Coatsworth. From SUMMER GREEN by Elizabeth Coatsworth. Copyright © 1948 by Macmillan Publishing Co., Inc. and renewed 1968 by Elizabeth Coatsworth Beston.

◆ Three Poems: Activity Sheet

(**Read and Understand**) Read the passage. Then answer these questions.

1. All three poems are about the same idea. What is it? _____

2. Which poem forgives March for blowing so much? _____

_____

3. Who is "you" in the poem by Mildred Pittinger? _____

_____

4. Think about the third poem. What is spring "winning"? _____

_____

(**Word Work: Synonyms**)

Look for synonyms in each poem. Circle them.

- ⟳ In "March" by Mildred Pittinger, find two synonyms. [Hint: Look in the first verse.]

- ⟳ In "Never Mind, March," find two synonyms for feeling cross.

- ⟳ In "March" by Elizabeth Coatsworth, find a synonym for *start*.

 Tip

Synonyms are words that mean the same thing.

Example:

cold and *chilly*

(**Check**) Circle the best choice.

Which word in one of the poems means the same as _frown_?

A. scowl   C. moan

B. blow   D. tear

Name _____   Date _____

 # Three Poems: Activity Sheet

Read and Understand) Read the passage. Then answer these questions.

1. What subject do all three poems describe? _____

2. Which poem imagines the job of making way for spring? _____

_____

3. Why does spring win a "battle" against winter in the poem by Elizabeth Coatsworth?

_____

4. Why does Mildred Pittinger say that March is part lion, part lamb?

_____

Word Work: Synonyms)

Fill in the charts. In each poem, find synonyms (words that mean the same thing)
for the words given.

"March" by Mildred Pittinger		"Never Mind, March"		"March" by Elizabeth Coatsworth	
hat	cap	understand		fine	
fellow		gust		start	
even-handed		truly		thawing	

Check) Circle the best choice.

Which word in one of the poems means the same as *stormy*?

A. blustery   C. quiet

B. melting   D. ready

Differentiated Activities for Teaching Key Comprehension Skills: Grades 2–3 © 2010 by Martin Lee and Marcia Miller. Scholastic Teaching Resources

Three Poems: Activity Sheet

Read and Understand Read the passage. Then answer these questions.

1. What subject do all three poems describe? _____

2. How does Mildred Pittinger use animals to describe March?

Explain what her idea means. _____

_____

3. Imagine how each poets feels. Which two poems give the sense that the harsh winds

of March are okay? _____

4. Why does Elizabeth Coatsworth mention birds in her poem? _____

_____

Word Work: Antonyms

Read each word in the first column. Reread the poem in the middle column.
Find the antonym for the given word. Write that antonym in the last column.

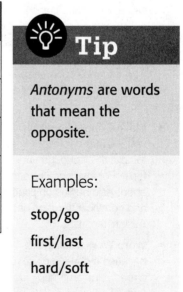

Words	Which Poem?	Antonym
quiet	"March," by Mildred Pittinger	
smile	"March," by Mildred Pittinger	
pay attention	"Never Mind, March"	
freezing	"March," by Elizabeth Coatsworth	
losing	"March," by Elizabeth Coatsworth	

Tip

Antonyms are words that mean the opposite.

Examples:

stop/go

first/last

hard/soft

Check Circle the best choice.

In which poem does every pair of lines rhyme?

A. "March," by Mildred Pittinger

B. "Never Mind, March"

C. "March," by Elizabeth Coatsworth

D. All three of them

Teaching **Meet a Book**

Students examine the title page and table of contents of a nonfiction book about dinosaurs.

Skills:

- Setting a purpose for reading
- Using text elements
- Making connections

Tasks	◆ Tier 1 Below Level	● Tier 2 On Level	⬟ Tier 3 Above Level
Set a purpose for reading	X	X	X
Identify and evaluate text elements	X	X	X
Make connections	X	X	X
Capitalize place names	X	X	
Identify main idea	X	X	X
Use word roots: *dict*			X

Getting Started

See the tips below for introducing the lesson. Make copies of the reading passage (pages 69–70) and the appropriate leveled activity sheet for each group of learners (pages 71–73).

Access prior knowledge about reasons for reading and setting a purpose for reading. Build background about common features found in nonfiction books, such as the table of contents and index.

 ## Tier 1

- **Text Elements:** Guide students to examine each element of the title page and table of contents. Help them notice bold text, italics, indentation, and page numbers, and talk about how these elements make it easier for readers to understand how the book is organized. Then work through items 1–3 together.

- **Make Connections:** Clarify that the number following each topic is the first page about that topic. For instance, the section about Asia begins on page 58 and continues through page 61. Assign item 4.

- **Word Work:** Distinguish between a generic place (e.g., a road), and a named place (e.g., Bell Road). Point out the capital letter that begins each place name. Extend by asking similar questions about local place names, helping students to write them correctly.

 ## Tier 2

- **Main Idea:** Ask students to make a connection between a chapter's title and its main idea. Then have students answer items 1 and 2. Compare and contrast the opening pages of this book with those of a fiction book about dinosaurs.

- **Text Elements:** See the first two bulleted items for Tier 1 for ideas. Then discuss item 3.

- **Make Connections:** For item 4, accept all reasonable responses. Have students explain the choices they made. Challenge them to explain why the second part of Chapter 5 is so much longer than the rest of the book. *(It is a dictionary-like listing of dinosaurs from A to Z.)*

- **Word Work:** Refer to the third bulleted item for Tier 1.

 ## Tier 3

- **Make Connections:** For items 1 and 2, challenge students to point to specific text elements that support their responses. Brainstorm different types of visual images that might appear in this book: drawings, fine art, photographs, diagrams, graphs.

- **Text Elements:** For item 3, accept all reasonable responses, asking students to explain their reasons. There are two possible answers for item 4; guide students to acknowledge both of them.

- **Word Work:** Other words with this root include *edict, verdict, diction, addict,* and *dictation*.

Meet a Book:
Reading Passage

Every book has a title page. Many books also have a table of contents.

Here are the title page and contents page for a new book.
Do you know someone who would like to read it?

All About Dinosaurs

Everything You've Always Wanted To Know

By Dr. Rex T. Rellick

Illustrations by Art Skelton

SCIENCE PUBLISHING COMPANY
Quarry, Montana

(continued)

Meet a Book: Reading Passage

(continued)

Contents

◆ Meet a Book: Activity Sheet

Read and Understand Read the passage. Then answer these questions.

1. Underline the title of the book.
Draw a box around the name of the author.
Circle the name of the person who drew the pictures.

2. How many chapters does this book have? _____

3. Which chapter lists dinosaurs from A to Z? _____

4. On which page does a section on museums begin? _____

Word Work: Place Names

Write each place name. Use a capital letter!

where the publisher is located _____

the first place name in Chapter 3 _____

the name of your state _____

> **Tip**
>
> Names of places always start with a capital letter. They are *proper nouns*.
>
> Examples:
>
> **Texas**
>
> **Japan**
>
> **Cedar City**

Check Circle the best choice.

What is the main idea of Chapter 2?

A. Cool Dino Data

B. Dinosaur Life

C. Dinosaurs Today

D. Dinosaurs Around the World

Meet a Book: Activity Sheet

(**Read and Understand**) Read the passage. Then answer these questions.

1. Is this book fiction or nonfiction? _____

How do you know? _____

2. What is Chapter 3 about? _____

3. What pages might describe dinosaurs in the film *Jurassic Park*? _____

4. You open the book to page 66. What might you see? _____

(**Word Work: Place Names**)

Write each place name. Be sure to use a capital letter.

where the publisher is located _____

the last place name in Chapter 3 _____

the name of your city or town _____

the name of your state _____

the name of the continent you live on _____

> **Tip**
>
> Names of places always start with a capital letter. They are *proper nouns*.
>
> Example:
>
> **Texas**   **Cedar City**
>
> **Japan**   **Jim's Cafe**

(**Check**) Circle the best choice.

Which pages are about how dinosaurs might be related to birds?

A. Pages 36–41

B. Pages 46–49

C. Pages 90–93

D. Pages 99–133

Name _____ Date _____

 # Meet a Book: Activity Sheet

Read and Understand Read the passage. Then answer these questions.

1. Is this book fiction or nonfiction? _____

How do you know? _____

2. What did Art Skelton do for this book? _____

3. If you open the book to page 60, what might you see? Give two ideas.

_____

_____

4. You loved the book *Danny and the Dinosaur,* by Syd Hoff.

What pages in *All About Dinosaurs* might mention it? _____

Word Work: Word Roots: dict

The root word **dict** means "say" or "speak." It comes from Latin.
Write the letter of the correct meaning next to **each** *dict* word.

_____ contradict   A. a leader who says what all the rules are

_____ dictate   B. to say what you think will happen

_____ dictator   C. to say the exact words you mean

_____ predict   D. to say the opposite

> **Tip**
>
> Dictionary is built on the word root *dict.* A dictionary lists in ABC order the words we say in our language.

Check Circle the best choice.

You want to read about the Zephyrosaurus.
Which page in *All About Dinosaurs* will most likely help you?

A. Page 132   C. Page 85

B. Page 99   D. Page 46

Reading Response Prompts

Making a Bird Feeder

◆ Thanks!
Pretend you are a hungry bird. Lucky for you, you found the new bird feeder. You had a lot to eat. Write a note to thank the person who made the feeder.

● Follow the Directions
Write a how-to piece for something simple you know how to do. Include an introduction, materials list, and steps.

⬠ Natural Crafts
Based on what you know about wildlife where you live, make a list of ideas for other projects you can make to help animals in your yard or a nearby park.

Clown Rounds

◆ Checkup
Think about a check-up you've had with a nurse or a doctor. Write about what happened. Describe what you had to do for the check-up.

● Express Yourself
Read the story out loud, saying each character's part with expression. Then write a sentence explaining which role you would want to play if you were acting it out. Don't forget the narrator!

⬠ To Clown or Not to Clown
Do you think it's a good idea for clowns to visit kids in the hospital? Some people love the idea. Others don't. Write a letter to the head of a hospital giving your opinion.

A Pair of Parties

◆ Make an Invitation
Think about a party you would like to have. Pick a date, time, and place. Make up an invitation you might send.

● Picking a Gift
How do you choose a gift for someone? Make a list of things you keep in mind.

⬠ Party Preference
Pretend you were invited to both parties you read about, but you could only go to one. Which party would you choose? Why? Write a description explaining your choice.

Teacher Boy

◆ Multiage School
Think about being in a class with kids of many ages. What would you like? What would you dislike? List your ideas in a T-chart.

● My School vs. Jack's School
Compare your school with the pioneer school. Make a T-chart. List things about your school on one side and about the pioneer school on the other.

⬠ Schools: Alike and Different
Use a Venn diagram to compare and contrast your school and the pioneer school. List similarities in the Both section. List differences in the outer part of each circle.

Rascal of the Ranch

◆ In the Audience
Imagine that you had a chance to see Skidboot perform. What do you think you would most enjoy? Write about being at a show.

● Dear David
Write a letter to David Hartwig telling him how you feel about Skidboot. You can send it to him at friends@skidboot.com.

⬠ Teaching a Dog
List ideas about training a dog. Then write three questions you have about teaching tricks to dogs. Speak to someone who has a dog or do research to answer the questions.

The Giant Hairy Toe

◆ The Giant's Version

Pretend you are the giant. Retell the part of the story about how you lost your toe. Write your story and share it with someone.

● Sounds of the Story

Think about what voices and sound effects you would use to make the story feel real. List the noises that you would add to each part of the story if it were acted on stage.

⬟ Family Folktales

Ask an adult family member to tell you a folktale he or she recalls from childhood. Then write your retelling of this story to share with classmates.

The Odd Echidna

◆ Echidna Reaction

Pretend you are an echidna. A large animal comes toward you. What do you do? Write about it.

● Echidna Comparison

Make a Venn diagram. Use it to compare the echidna to another mammal you know, such as a dog, rabbit, hamster, or horse. Show how the two mammals are different and alike.

⬟ Echidna Facts

Make a poster about the echidna. Use drawings, facts, and other details to help others learn about this odd mammal.

Goal!

◆ Character Clues

Choose one of the four characters in the play. Think of everything you can imagine about that character, including looks, clothes, speech, and habits. Write your ideas.

● I Want to Direct!

Pretend that you are a director putting on this play. What costumes, props, and scenery would you need? How would you tell the actors to say their lines? Write your ideas.

⬟ Scene Two

Write another scene for the same four characters. Pretend that they are at the pizza place with Hannah and her coach. Write lines that each character might say.

Amber

◆ Paint a Picture in Your Mind

Based on what you read and saw, picture a piece of amber. Describe it as best you can. Then find a color photo of amber in a book or online, with the help of an adult.

● Gemstones

Write about other gemstones you know. With adult help, do research to find the names and colors of other gemstones. Make a poster to share this information.

⬟ More About Amber

With an adult, find a color photo of amber in a book or online. Then write a poem about what you see when you look at amber and how it makes you feel.

Three Poems

◆ Many Views of March

Write your own poem about the month of March. Feel free to take some ideas from the poems you've read, but use your own strong words and special language.

● Another Month

Pick a month of the year you like. Think of ways to describe that month in a poem. Use one of the three poems as a model, or come up with your own idea.

⬟ Images of the Month

Think about an image for each month of the year. It might include a holiday, weather, or whatever else makes sense to you. For example, "July is firecracker time...." List the images in calendar order.

Meet a Book

◆ Comparing Books

Find a nonfiction book on dinosaurs. Compare and contrast its title page and table of contents with the one from this passage. Use a Venn diagram to write your ideas.

● Book Look

Choose a nonfiction book from the library. Figure out what the book is about. How is it organized? What parts does it have? Who might enjoy it? Write your ideas.

⬟ Fiction vs. Nonfiction

Pick a fiction book you have not read. Preview it. What clues can you find on the book jacket and title page? What do the illustrations tell you? Write your preview ideas.

Answer Key

Making a Bird Feeder

Tier 1, page 11:
Read and Understand: 1. how to make a bird feeder 2. Students should circle the materials list: string or twine, butter knife, birdseed, pinecone, vegetable shortening, foil or waxed paper. 3. 6; to show the correct order to do the steps 4. Students should underline Step 2

Word Work: from, up, near, with

Check: C

Tier 2, page 12:
Read and Understand: 1. how to make a bird feeder 2. You Need 3. Step 2 4. It is covered with birdseed

Word Work: from, up, near, out, around

Check: B

Tier 3, page 13:
Read and Understand: 1. It tells exactly how to make a bird feeder 2. gather the items shown 3. to make a loop for hanging the bird feeder 4. It is covered with birdseed

Word Work: Sentences will vary; check student work

Check: B

Clown Rounds

Tier 1, page 17:
Read and Understand: 1. Dr. Tickles and Nurse Boo-Boo 2. He was having an operation; to cheer him up 3. Check students' choices. 4. Paragraph that begins "Squish," and the next one

Word Work: He, It, she, They

Check: C

Tier 3, page 18:
Read and Understand: 1. He was having an operation; to cheer him up 2. His coat has patches, he wears purple glasses, a blue wig, and a red nose; his name is funny 3. Her name is funny, her shoes squeak, she wears a silly baseball cap, holds a giant balloon needle, and squirts a lemon 4. Both try to make you feel better; both wear special outfits

Word Work: She, He, It, They

Check: C

Tier 3, page 19:
Read and Understand: 1. He was having an operation; to cheer him up 2. He honks a horn; he uses a stethoscope on Toby's arm; he makes Toby a balloon hat; he does magic tricks 3. Her name is funny, her shoes squeak, and she wears a baseball cap, holds a giant balloon needle, and squirts a lemon 4. Both try to make you feel better; both wear special outfits

Word Work: She, He, It, They

Check: C

A Pair of Parties

Tier 1, page 23:
Read and Understand: 1. Diana; Duquan 2. July 14 and July 13; Duquan's 3. Circle fifth paragraph 4. Duquan's

Word Work: Students should circle Diana; Poppy Rd.; State St.; The Pizza Palace; Sunday, Friday, Saturday, Wednesday

Check: D

Answer Key *(continued)*

Tier 2, page 24:
Read and Understand: 1. at home; out
2. Duquan's 3. It is the last house on the left;
has balloons in front; is #53 on Poppy Rd.
4. a root beer float that Diana's mother makes

Word Work: Diana; Poppy Rd.; State St.; The
Pizza Palace; Any of the following: Sunday,
Friday, Saturday, Wednesday

Check: C

Tier 3, page 25:
Read and Understand: 1. Diana Duquan
2. Wednesday 3. Diana's; Diana's 4. Duquan's

Word Work: Mister/Mr., Street/St., Doctor/Dr.,
Wednesday/Wed., Building/Bldg

Check: C

Teacher Boy

Tier 1, page 29:
Read and Understand: 1. Students should circle
two text clues in the passage, such as: *That was
the only book Jake had; It was Emma's first year of
schooling. She was eight; First came chores; He asked
Seth to fill the bucket. Jake and Emma were pioneer
kids; My horse went lame and couldn't pull my
wagon. Miss Colter untied her bonnet and hung it on
a nail.* 2. Answers should refer to the size of the
schools, activities in class, features of the school's
simple inside. 3. The teacher was not there; Jake
became the teacher. 4. They respected her; she
was a lady.

Word Work: didn't, you're, it's, isn't

Check: C

Tier 2, page 30:
Students should circle three text clues in the
passage, such as: *That was the only book Jake had;
It was Emma's first year of schooling. She was eight;
First came chores; He asked Seth to fill the bucket.
Jake and Emma were pioneer kids; My horse went
lame and couldn't pull my wagon. Miss Colter untied
her bonnet and hung it on a nail.* 2. Students
should refer to size of school, activities done in
school, features the school's simple inside. 3. He
helped get started because the teacher was not
there; He didn't want the other kids to have to
wait and get worried. 4. They respected her; she
was a lady.

Word Work: does not, you are, it is, have not

Check: C

Tier 3, page 31:
Read and Understand: 1. Students should circle
three text clues in the passage, such as: *That was
the only book Jake had; It was Emma's first year
of schooling. She was eight; First came chores; He
asked Seth to fill the bucket. Jake and Emma were
pioneer kids; My horse went lame and couldn't pull
my wagon. Miss Colter untied her bonnet and hung
it on a nail.* 2. Answers will vary; check student
responses. 3. The teacher was not there; he
became the teacher 4. The students began to
behave; They felt relieved and happy to go back
to a regular day.

Word Work: you're, we're, it's, didn't

Check: C

Rascal of the Ranch

Tier 1, page 35:
Read and Understand: 1. He's a rascal, and
he lives on a ranch. 2. "It's not hard work if
you enjoy it." 3. He needed a gift for his wife.
4. He learned and did many great tricks.

Word Work blue, school, shoe, who, you

Check: D

Tier 2, page 36:
Read and Understand: 1. Sample answer:
I thought I would read about a ranch and a
character who acts like a rascal, but I wasn't sure
if it was a person or animal. 2. "It's not hard
work if you enjoy it." 3. He watched carefully

and copied what he saw. 4. Sample answer: to inform people about an amazing dog

Word Work: knew; true; school; shoe; hoop

Check: B

Tier 3, page 37:
Read and Understand: 1. Sample answer: to inform people about an amazing dog 2. He got into trouble on the ranch. 3. He watched carefully and copied what he saw. 4. "It's not hard work if you enjoy it."

Word Work: Sample answers: moo, zoo, boo, goo; true, clue, glue; stew, grew, chew, threw; zoom, groom, broom

Check: B

The Giant Hairy Toe

Tier 1, page 41:
Read and Understand: 1. a poor old woman and a giant; Check student drawings. 2. The story takes place in a hut deep in the woods, far from town; no, it just says "once upon a time" 3. She had finally eaten meat for a meal; Check student markings. 4. They would snuggle close together to feel safe

Word Work: went; But the creatures of the woods went on alert; saw; She saw an odd lump by the fence; ate; The old woman ate three bowls

Check: B

Tier 2, page 42:
Read and Understand: 1. It takes place in a tiny hut in the woods; Sample answer: I think it happened long ago. 2. She couldn't move at all, as if she became ice. 3. Sample answer: The giant was searching for his lost toe. Maybe the giant remembered losing it in the old woman's garden or smelled the hairy toe soup. 4. Sample answer: The giant ate her or carried her away

Word Work: She bends down for a closer look; So she takes the hairy toe back to her hut; She holds her pillow over her ears

Check: D

Tier 3, page 43:
Read and Understand: 1. Sample answer: Being alone deep in dark woods on a stormy night in a tiny hut that offers little protection are all elements that work for this kind of scary folktale. 2. She was hungry and hadn't had meat in a long time. 3. Sample answers: They build suspense, give you the creeps, make you want to read on, spark your imagination. 4. empty, dull, flat, without emotion

Word Work: barefoot; bare + foot; a foot that is bare; without shoes; floorboards; floor + boards; boards used to make a floor; nobody; no + body; not even one body (no person)

Check: C

The Echidna

Tier 1, page 47:
Read and Understand: 1. Sample answer: What makes an echidna odd? 2. Students should circle the following sentences: *All mammals share key traits. Here are some of them.* 3. Australia. 4. a baby echidna; it is a new word; italics helps it stand out

Word Work: mother's; echidna's; nature's

Check: D

Tier 2, page 48:
Read and Understand: 1. Sample answer: What makes an echidna odd? 2. Students should circle the following: *Picture some of an echidna's surprising features:* 3. It has legs and claws. It likes to sniff. 4. Possible answers: It has spines.

It has a pouch. It is a mammal but lays eggs. It curls into a ball.

Word Work: mother's; mother; echidna's; echidna; nature's; nature

Check: D

Tier 3, page 49:

Read and Understand: 1. Sample answer: What makes an echidna odd? 2. Possible answer: The text inside parentheses adds more information. 3. The author is giving examples that support why the echidna is so odd. 4. Both lay eggs; the echidna cannot fly.

Word Work: strongest, the most strong, She is the strongest swimmer; smallest, the most small; I ate the smallest cookie; warmest, the most warm; Wear your warmest jacket.

Check: B

Goal!

Tier 1, page 53:

Read and Understand: 1. Mom, Tim, Lia, Nate 2. Check setting line at the beginning of the play 3. The Lemons 4. He told Lia that his coach knew Lia was a strong player, and urged the team to keep her from scoring.

Word Work: Check students' papers.

Check: D

Tier 2, page 54:

Read and Understand: 1. They tell the name of the character who says the words on that line. 2. in a car, going home after a soccer game 3. Nate; There are clues in lines 7, 17, 21, and 30. Students should circle two of these lines. 4. Hannah is usually the high scorer on the Lemons; they talk about her because she scored the only goal.

Word Work: grate/great; two/too; know/no; fair/fare

Check: C

Tier 3, page 55:

Read and Understand: 1. In a play, a character's name appears at the beginning of each line he or she speaks. 2. They are stage directions, or hints, that tell characters how to act when saying that line. 3. In a car, going home after a soccer game 4. Last time, Lia's team let the Lemons score four goals, but this time the Lemons scored only one goal.

Word Work: great; team; know; fair; not

Check: C

Amber

Tier 1, page 59:

Read and Understand: 1. Students should circle paragraph 3; sticky, like syrup 2. Students should circle the sentence in paragraph 7: *They study it to learn about life on earth long ago.* 3. It is the color of the sun, and it is smooth and hard, like something frozen.

Word Work: Check student clues.

Check: C

Tier 2, page 60:

Read and Understand: 1. Students should circle paragraph 3; Resin seals cracks, fills in holes, and keeps out germs. 2. They study it to learn about life on earth long ago. 3. It is smooth, like ice you find in the north, and it is gold in color.

Word Work: cure, valuable, links, seal

Check: C

Tier 3, page 61:

Read and Understand: 1. Students should circle paragraph 3: It seals cracks, fills in holes, and keeps out germs. 2. Scientists study the fossils trapped in amber to learn more about ancient life on earth. 3. Answers will vary. Check student responses

Word Work: Sentences will vary.

Check: C

Three Poems

Tier 1, page 65:

Read and Understand: 1. the month of March 2. "Never Mind, March" 3. the month of March 4. Spring is winning the battle against winter.

Word Work: Students should circle the following words: *loud*, *noisy*; *mad*, *angry*; *beginning*

Check: A

Tier 2, page 66:

Read and Understand: 1. the month of March 2. "Never Mind, March" 3. In March, the winter snow starts to melt. 4. This means that March is both wild like a lion and gentle like a lamb

Word Work: cap, chap, fair; know, blow, really; good, beginning, melting

Check: A

Tier 3, page 67:

Read and Understand: 1. the month of March 2. She says that March is part lion, part lamb. This means that March is both wild like a lion and gentle like a lamb. 3. the first two poems 4. In spring birds make nests and have babies

Word Work: loud/noisy; scowl; never mind; melting; winning

Check: B

Meet a Book

Tier 1, page 71:

Read and Understand: 1. On the title page, students should underline the title: *All About Dinosaurs*, box the author's name: *Dr. Rex T. Rellick*, and circle the illustrator's name: *Art Skelton*. 2. five 3. five 4. 78

Word Work: Quarry, Montana; Africa; Check that students have listed your state

Check: B

Tier 2, page 72:

Read and Understand: 1. nonfiction; It gives facts and information on dinosaurs. 2. dinosaurs that lived in different places in the world 3. 94–97 4. Sample answers: a map of Europe; pictures of fossils or dinosaurs found in Europe

Word Work: Quarry, Montana; South America; Check that students have listed your town or city, state, and continent

Check: C

Tier 3, page 73:

Read and Understand: 1. nonfiction; It gives facts and information on dinosaurs. 2. He is the illustrator; he worked on the art to go with the text 3. a map of Asia; pictures of fossils or dinosaurs found in Asia 4. 94–97

Word Work: D; C; A; B

Check: A